THE NEW LEFT CHURCH

TERENCE EAGLETON

The
New Left
Church

HELICON
BALTIMORE

FIRST PUBLISHED 1966
HELICON PRESS, INC.
1120 N. CALVERT STREET
BALTIMORE, MARYLAND 21202

Library of Congress Catalog Card Number 66–24850

This book is set in 11 pt. Linotype Baskerville

Made and printed in Great Britain by
William Clowes and Sons, Limited, London and Beccles

Contents

Foreword

All the essays in this book are concerned with the church, literature and politics. This structure is part of the meaning of each chapter: the implicit claim is that, for a Christian, no one strand of the web which links these three concerns can be touched without affecting the others. The web image isn't perfect, because some movements within this web seem easier than others: it is easier for Christians to move between church, culture and politics than for non-Christians to move through culture and politics into the church. But this is not particularly important, as the aim of the book isn't to convert agnostic politicians, but to persuade Christians that being in the church involves commitment to imaginative culture and the political left.

These last two areas have been linked for a long time, independently of Christians. The relation between imaginative creation and political radicalism is a traditional one in Britain; both are concerned with kinds of energy which a philistine capitalism is felt to deny, both identify a human wholeness which is being fragmented.

The tradition comes through from men like William Morris and D. H. Lawrence to the cultural and political thinkers of our own time, the writers and critics of the New Left in Britain. To be involved in culture now is to be involved in politics; to look for an adequate politics is to be concerned with the arts. What the church, the arts and politics have in common is that they all offer basic descriptions of what it is to be human. The argument of this book is that these come, finally, to the same description.

Christians are beginning, slowly, to see their place in the web; to see where their theology meshes with politics, where ideas of grace and charity link with literary truths and social programmes. One nodal point where the strands are drawn together is in the idea of *culture*: here we have the term which mediates each concern into the other, deepening our understanding of the church through literary insight and translating this into commitment within society. Or, conversely, deepening our understanding of politics through Christian insight and doing this in terms of literature: all movement within the web comes to the same centre.

F. R. Leavis drew together some of the strands in his Richmond lecture of 1962:

> ... the advance of science and technology means a human future of change so rapid and of such kinds, of tests and challenges so unprecedented, of decisions and possible non-

decisions so momentous and insidious in their consequences, that mankind—this is surely clear—will need to be in full intelligent possession of its full humanity (and "possession" here means, not confident ownership of that which belongs to *us*—our property—but a basic living deference towards that to which, opening as it does into the unknown and itself immeasurable, we know we belong)...What we need, and shall continue to need not less, is something with the livingness of the deepest vital instinct; an intelligence, a power—rooted, strong in experience, and supremely human—of creative response to the new challenges of time...

The "basic living deference", the reverence, is shared equally by the Christian, the artist, and the radical humanist. Dr Leavis's paradox, of a supreme human affirmation which in this very act knows itself as belonging to a depth beyond it, is the Christian's paradox too, belonging to God by being most fully himself; it is also the paradox of the radical humanist, who affirms the conscious human power to change society on the grounds of a reverence for human life which goes deeper than conscious possession. If the Christian responds to the Spirit in a great novel he is responding to what is centrally human in it; to say, after the resurrection, that the poet is divine is to say he is in touch with what is most real in human life. To identify what is real, which actions make for life, is to be politically committed; here the "deepest vital instinct" is measured against an actual society, actual structures and relationships. Not to make this link is to leave the insights abstract; it is this connection—the one Christians have been traditionally so reluctant to make in any detail—which makes sense of all other connections. This book is an attempt to correct the traditional imbalance by showing that our statements about the church and culture are also political statements, part of a radical assault on our society whether they know themselves as this or not.

I would like to thank various friends whose influence and ideas have been important to me in writing this book, especially Laurence Bright, OP, Herbert McCabe, OP, Adrian Cunningham, and Brian Wicker, whose *Culture and Liturgy* has been a seminal work in this whole field. I dedicate this book to Rosemary Galpin, who read all the chapters as they were written, and whose involvement and enthusiasm have been my chief encouragement in writing.

Jesus College, Cambridge
October 1965

1

The New Left church

Much of the discussion to date of what can broadly be called the "New Left church" has centred on the idea of the liturgy, and its function in fostering the growth of a new society. I think this is a very valuable approach, and perhaps the ultimate terms in which to put the case, but I think also that before dealing with the question of how we make the difficult relation between the values we find enacted in the liturgical community and those we want to see generally prevalent, we have to face the more basic problem of whether there isn't anyway an unresolved contradiction in the whole idea of Christians claiming to talk about society. By "society" I mean in particular the ordinary processes of living in community, and the institutions which shape these processes; and in talking about these, the Christian faces a difficulty which grows from the peculiar nature of his belief. For the Christian, in claiming to speak relevantly about society, is making the large claim of uniting two bodies of feeling which much modern experience suggests to be incompatible: the idea of the common life, and the idea of intensity. I think we have to examine this suggested incompatibility first, and see whether from this we can get an idea of what a Christian society would look like.

It seems obvious, to begin with, that Christianity is an extremist belief, extreme and uncompromising in its tolerance and love. William Golding put this well in *Pincher Martin*, when he described the black lightning of God which burnt away Martin's resistance as having "a compassion that was timeless and without mercy". We have to be totally committed to Christ, and any total commitment is potentially tragic because it blocks off one of the only ways we know out of tragedy, the way of compromise. Christianity sets itself against compromise and half-measure; it tells us to pluck out eyes and walk two miles instead of one, and it is part of the nature of any total demand on a man's energies that it contains the power to break him. Sometimes there comes a point where the man has to be broken to answer the demand, where he can only attain the wholeness he looks for in the process of being smashed. This is a common enough situation in tragedy: Ibsen's Master Builder chooses to fall from the top of a tower rather than to live without ever having climbed, Willy Loman in Arthur Miller's *Death of a Salesman* goes to his death rather than walk away from the commitment with which his very identity is involved. In the act of staying committed, in the refusal to walk away, Miller's characters experience a wholeness and intensity which is very close to the Christian experience: the idea of martyrdom is often there, as an undertone. But Miller, at least, has no answer to the problem of how to reconcile common living with an intensity of commitment which breaks through it. At the end of *A View from the Bridge*, after Eddie Carbone has destroyed himself by his ruthless refusal to back down from the problem of his own life, the lawyer Alfieri finishes the play with these words:

> Most of the time now we settle for half, and I like that better. But the truth is holy, and even as I know how wrong he was, and his death useless, I tremble, for something perversely pure calls to me from his memory: not purely good, but himself purely, for he allowed himself to be fully known, and for that I shall like him better than all my sensible clients. And yet, it is better to settle for half, it must be! And so I mourn him, I confess, with a certain ... alarm.

Eddie Carbone was wrong, objectively, in his commitment; he was driven by a false version of reality, and he is both a madman and a hero. The tragedy is that, in a compromising society, the movement to wholeness and integrity involves a destructiveness, of oneself and others, which is both fanatical and Christlike. When all the voices are calling for compromise, when Willy Loman's neighbours are telling him to settle for half, Loman himself stands by his demand for recognition from a false society, and the intensity of his commitment becomes an isolating force, it moves him ever further from the society into which he is trying to become integrated. The triumph and the blindness of Willy Loman is that although the capitalist society he lives in is so clearly incapable of providing the recognition he needs, he never turns away from it—he presses his impossible demands through to the end and is destroyed by them. He dies without ever having known who he was, but the truth and the wholeness lie in the intensity of his energy.

This seems to me, for Christians, one of the crucial paradoxes of modern experience, and any thinking about society we do has to take this into account. Willy Loman is fanatically committed to verification by his society, the more the society ignores him the more fanatical he becomes, and thus the further alienated he is. The society lacks his capacity for tragic experience—he is superior, in intensity, to it; his refusal to compromise is a dangerous and holy force, one which opens him fully to society, which renders him totally vulnerable and speeds his destruction. Like Eddie Carbone, he allows himself to be fully known, and this is inadvisable in a society sold over to the ethic of privacy. Intensity moves a man out of community, even when it is directed towards his integration—it gives men a thirst for the whole truth which makes them dangerous. The same problem occurs in Miller's *All My Sons*, where the son, Chris, has to choose between pressing home his commitment to discovering the truth of his father's concealed crime and thus destroying him, or slackening his grip and accepting half-measure. Chris's answer, to the mother who pleads for tolerance and compromise, is that if a new world is to be established at all it will need an act of fanaticism to do it: there has to be a point where the circuit is broken, where the lies and half-measures are smashed into truth, and men may die in the process. It's the problem we face in Ibsen's *Brand*, where we feel safe in our condemnation of Brand's inhuman demand for total integrity until we see that the alternative might be the shifty and deceitful compromise of the Provost.

Miller and Ibsen point to the general dilemma: how is intensity to be fed creatively into a society, how are we to stop it tearing through the fabric of the common life? This was Lawrence's problem, too: part of the tragedy of Lawrence is that intensities of personal feeling which were at some point, or are still at some level, being offered as model feelings and values for a new society, gain by the very fact of being offered outside the context of a sustaining society, in the medium of literature only, a quality which is hostile not only to a specific capitalist society, but to the whole idea of the common life and ordinary living: one lapses away from this into a personal intensity, the material detail and clutter is cleared out of the way to leave room for this powerful inward living.

As Christians we are committed to the idea of intensity, we live as potential martyrs, and yet we are also claiming to have something to contribute to the problem of how men should commonly live in society. This, as I have said, is an unusual claim, one going against the grain of modern experience—and one obvious way out is to drop either side of the equation, to deny that the Christian experience should be one of intensity, or to deny that we are committed to a whole society. If we do the former we stand with Dostoyevsky's Grand Inquisitor in condemning Christ for demanding superhuman responses— we accept the fact that to condemn big business or nuclear weapons might be expedient; on the other hand, few Christians would now want to deny their involvement in a whole society. We can get a fuller idea of what intensity means by going back to Golding's phrase about the ruthlessness of God's compassion: God's love batters Pincher Martin to pieces, it can't be resisted, and Martin's response is one of hatred for this force, totally inhuman in its persistence. Something of the same feeling comes across in Graham Greene's *The Heart of the Matter*, where Scobie's response to the crucifix in the church is one of irritation at God's vulgarity in suffering in public. God is insistent beyond the bounds of common politeness, he crops up in the interstices of every feeling and relationship with impudent and shameless regularity: he's there to the end, tapping around outside the house where Scobie lies dying, crying to come in, grovelling before his creatures, totally vulnerable. This is irritating to Scobie, because he has been educated in a society where persistence and vulnerability are both signs of bad breeding: vulnerability is taboo because too many people are out to wound, and so the men at the club live shut off from each other, tucking their secrets out of sight; persistence is also taboo, because it shows a sort of fanatical inability to accept what is to Greene the inevitable half-measure of life, the necessary breakdown and deceit and compromise. It seems to suggest that life can be lived with a wholeness, and it's because Greene sometimes mistakes this wholeness for a kind of mathematical accuracy that he flings the mess and complexity of life back in God's face, trying to wound his geometrical mind with the facts of human imprecision. For Greene, intensity and common living can't generally be reconciled—intensity is a sign of innocence and thus of insanity; human beings can never really live out the ruthless love of their Creator.

And yet the christian life must have this absolutism. On this let me quote Herbert

McCabe: "The fire of hell is God. God is terrible and no man can look on him and live, he is a consuming fire. To be safe in the presence of God you must yourself be sacred, you must share in God's power and life."[1] Through grace, then, we are filled with something of God's extremism and ruthlessness: the command to love is absolute, and potentially destructive. All christians must be martyrs, they must die physically in Christ, and the moment of death, according to St Paul and T. S. Eliot, is every moment—we live in a state of perfectedness. There is something unusual of course in defining how we should live by reference to the experience of dying, and the difficulty comes out in T. S. Eliot's work. In Eliot's plays, martyrdom is the central experience, and it has a depth which puts it in some way out of time, fixes it at the still point of the turning world. For Eliot the moment of death is every moment; but the difficulty in showing how people ought to live by highlighting the moment of death becomes obvious once you put the thing on stage, since the death unfortunately removes the central character from our sight and leaves us wondering just what kind of life he would have made for himself, in terms of the ordinary world, if he could have gone on living with the intensity which takes him off-stage. Thomas in *Murder in the Cathedral* goes to heaven, Celia in *The Cocktail Party* to Africa, and this, though

[1] H. McCabe, *The New Creation*, London 1964, 189.

impressive, still leaves us with the problem of what happens to the people left in the turning world who didn't quite make the still point: what kind of life or intensity is possible for them? For Eliot, the difficulty resolves itself to some extent by the fact that he doesn't anyway think that these people are really capable of living their lives with the intensity of death—they are common women or shallow *bourgeois,* and a partial living in the "twittering world" of Putney and Highgate and all those other vulgar places is about the best they can manage. So he absolves himself, neatly, from the problem of demonstrating how the intensity of Thomas can be channelled back into society, of showing what kind of community could grow out of it.

The received attitude to the common life in Britain since the industrial revolution has been to devaluate it: this is a dangerous generalisation, but it is very nearly true. George Eliot chose to write novels about Midlands rural communities and then spent half her time in the novels apologising for it. For her, in *Adam Bede,* Methodism had a positive value in injecting into the common life an intensity of feeling which was normally alien to it, but this rested on the suspicion that the common detail of life was something intrinsically inferior, and that a touch of irony in the tone was essential to convey this suspicion to the reader. Dorothea Brooke in *Middlemarch* dreams of a pure act, intense and martyrlike, and this alienates her from the community; at the end of the novel she returns from this intense reaching for self-fulfilment to the common life of her society: "her full nature ... spent itself in channels which had no great name on the earth". But to Eliot, what a feeling gains by its widespread diffusion into the fabric of a community it loses in the thinning of its intensity: the return to community is, perhaps, a settling for half, a downpedalling of intensity to the level at which the routine life of a society can sustain it.

Intensity takes men outside the community: this has been a recurrent theme in modern experience. For E. M. Forster, the business of connecting the prose of common living with the passion of the intense moment is a continuing and fruitless struggle; for Virginia Woolf, the inner and outer worlds are ripped apart, events in the public world are chopped up and interspersed as small asides and subordinate clauses in a stream of glowing inwardness. The routine comic experience of our time has been that of Tony Hancock, with his sudden juxtapositions of rhetoric and slang; we are at a stage where any value or feeling or attitude can seem to be refuted merely by reference to the texture of ordinary living. This is so in Chehov, for example, where even though what we are seeing is clearly a tragic society, none of the characters dare say so, because to take any kind of formu-lated position, to strike the posture necessary just to make a general statement, is felt to falsify; if one character uses the word "tragedy" somebody else is bound to try and argue that it's just the room temperature that's too high. This, indeed, is part of the tragic experience in Chehov—the fact that it's really impossible to have one, to take refuge either in the monotony of ordinary life or in the intensity of a tragic response. Most of the characters are stranded somewhere between.

As Christians then, we are using intensity as an instrument for judging men and societies; we are saying that actions and cultures which fall below the degree of commitment we look for in our own lives are to be seen as inferior. We are also, more subtly, demanding that, for wholeness, a man or society must be capable of experiencing tragedy, because it is the tragic experience which the Christian must prepare for: he must pray to avoid the test, because when the test comes it may break him—and this seems to me still a tragic thing, even though the result of the breaking might be an achieved wholeness. But holding up the tragic experience as a criterion in this way is a dangerous process—one that can lead in practice to the familiar opposing of tragedy and society, tragedy and common life. In Sartre and Unamuno, for instance, the tragic insight is a way of defining oneself as authentic against the blindness of the herd, the *bourgeois* in their little boxes—and this sort of judgement nearly always involves that particular kind of crude and arrogant categorisation. We sometimes get the assertion that the outsider wants to re-integrate, and yet at the same time he clings to his superior insight—he mustn't lose hold of this and be absorbed. The solution then is clearly to say that one will reintegrate with a changed society, but by this time the tragic insight is often inseparable from a whole sense of oneself as a lone individual, which makes community on any terms very difficult. One has defined oneself so positively as an outsider in relation to a specific *bourgeois* society that the feelings and values this generates then become part of one's general description of oneself, and opposition to *bourgeois* society therefore slides, sometimes only subconsciously, into opposition to *any* society. Tragedy, intensity, is still something which can only exist outside society, which defines itself in contradistinction to the common life.

The Christian has to find some way of resolving this problem, of sustaining simultaneously a care for the integrity of the Christian experience and a care for the creation of a decent common life. We can get some understanding of how intensity and common life are reconciled through our whole developing sense of the continuum of sacred and secular which Christ effected in the world—the gathering up of the common life, of bread and water and our ordinary relations with others, into the intensity of the divine life. In this way the obvious area in which sacred and secular, the intense and the ordinary, are fused, is in the liturgy itself, where the objects and relationships should keep their ordinary meanings and functions in terms of the human community, and yet are part of a greater intensity of life. We are looking, in other words, for a society which is in this sense sacramental, where the ordinary processes of living can themselves be part of a depth, having a living relation to beliefs and values.

This is a generally revolutionary position, because the point of a capitalist society is that the ordinary processes of life and production become so progressively meaningless that people are forced to turn for their living elsewhere—to the arts or the pub or personal relationships. We see this dichotomy in the twentieth-century novel, which shows a serious dislocation of its deepest levels of life from the ordinary process of living, and where the movement from one to the other presents itself as a movement from intensity to sordid routine, from the inward to the external. How to make the common life significant is a central problem here: we can resort to the subconscious, like Iris Murdoch, or stylise and intensify breakfast-table conversation like Ivy Compton-Burnett, or twist the surfaces of events until they deflect just enough meaning for one's moral pattern, like William Golding; but the problem refuses to be twisted or stylised away, it remains as a flaw at the heart of our experience. In the liturgy we have the prototype of how we might resolve this: we see that our ordinary Christian living must have a wholeness which isn't incompatible with the detailed processes of living—rather that the wholeness forms through our concern with the details.

This, in practice, would mean a society where the common life of work was sacramental in the sense that it shaped and affirmed a human community, where the means for entering into the most intense experience the society had to offer were the normal means of life and production, and the common culture which grew from this economic community. The point of ordinary family life is, of course, that the economic relationships of man, wife, and child can't be separated from the mutual love; each grows in terms of the other, and any dislocation is fatal. And so if we can attack, with Carlyle and Ruskin, the loveless cash-nexus of capitalist society, we can also justly ask what all those people in some of Lawrence's novels *do* all day when they aren't making love. Similarly, in the liturgy we don't, or shouldn't, abandon our normal human and economic relationships, and it is part of the deformity of the liturgy in a capitalist society that we have to suppress our just hostility to the stockbroker taking the eucharist at our elbow, and see him artificially in two different personae.

This sense of the importance of building a just material community, and the coincidence of this building with the intensity of our Christian lives, doesn't seem to be there fully in the work of most of our progressive theologians. It's present to an extent, of course; but the final commitment—the fact that it's only in terms of our commitment to the building of this community that we can, at this point in time, be fully attuned to the creative movement of salvation history—is still resisted. Jean Daniélou, in his discussion of Marxist and sacramental history in the *Lord of History*, and Karl Rahner in his treatment of individual and society in *Mission and Grace* (vol. 1), both withhold this final commitment. Yes, Christianity is something social and material, but in the final analysis it is something beyond these, a different order, and the two orders never quite coincide. Rahner seems to see the highest, most authentic and individual, acts of spirituality as "acts which, of their very nature, cannot be compelled from without by the suggestings and conditionings of education, of so-called public opinion, of advertising, of infection from other psyches or by the 'masses' ".[1] The significance of that "compelled from without", with its Cartesian dualism, the mechanistic coldness of "infection from other psyches" and "masses", are clear enough: we live freshly and spontaneously from a centre which is

[1] K. Rahner, *Mission and Grace*, I, London 1963, 132.

ultimately beyond the reach of the clutter of social mechanism. This mechanism is indeed part of our totality, and thus enters into the Christian experience—but this in context is a reservation. The most authentic living is done from the untouched spiritual centre.

Rahner has of course an important point in his sense of living and acting from this centre, and it is this which we can most usefully put beside what we are taught by writers like D. H. Lawrence. While Christian theologians are understanding grace as a spontaneous living freed from law and mechanical habit, Lawrence, too, is developing a sense of spontaneous-creative life, in the context of a society which is closed to it. With both Rahner and Lawrence, spontaneity can be a dangerous way of sidestepping actual social commitment, and the Christian's task is to translate the emphasis into actual terms: to fuse the intensity of spontaneous living with the common detail of social life. By turning to the idea of socialism, we find that the dual commitment which we have seen as a difficulty in Christian thinking may in fact be a strength. It gives us a wholeness of concern, a simultaneity of emphasis, at a time when socialism needs to be healed in precisely this way—to regain a sense of its human depth while realising itself as a practical force. We have precedents for doing this to which we can turn, in men like William Morris, who succeeded more than anyone in translating the intensity of art into the terms of a common life, in seeing what the experience of writing poetry could tell you about the nature of factory work. I think that it is in some direction of this kind that Christian radical thinking has to go: it must be careful, in regaining a sense of the depth and intensity of what it means to be a Christian, of shaking off liberal compromise and middle-of-the-road solutions, to arrive at the position of a William Morris and not, as can happen too, of a Walter Pater; the intensity has to be explored within the context of a whole concern, not set up as a rival to common experience. Morris saw that running a factory was as much a continuous work of the imagination as painting a picture, and we can appeal from this to the words of William Carlos Williams, who asked, simply: "Are not facts flowers, and flowers facts, and poems flowers, and all works of the imagination, interchangeable?"

So far we have talked about intensity and spontaneity, but now we must see in more detail what these mean in terms of the Christian life, and whether from these we can develop a political position which is genuinely Christian, tackling the urgent issues of capitalism and nuclear weapons. To begin with, it is necessary to examine the Christian idea of equality, because this is often something we seem to take for granted in the abstract, without close scrutiny. It seems obvious that when the Christian talks about equality he means something different from what the humanist means, and it is this difference which is immediately interesting. We tend often to think of equality as being so because God made us like that, sharing a common condition, and this of course is true; but more concretely we are equals because we live, not with our own lives, but with the Christ-life which we manifest, and equality therefore means unity in Christ: things which share the same life are equal, they share the same value. It is easy to see how this is so in the Christian community, but we have to remember also that all creation is permeated by the Christ-life, showing it forth, and for the Christian things take their being from this source. Mountains show forth the Christ-life, not in the facile sense of the pathetic fallacy, but because, as Wordsworth understood, in learning to see and describe and respond to a mountain its significance in the human pattern slowly grows, even while it retains its unique selfhood. And so as Christians we see objects and human beings simultaneously as autonomous beings and as related outwards, part of a deeper pattern. There's always a tension in this—always a necessity to resist seeing objects and people and situations merely as signs and emblems of the divine life, or seeing them as unrelated, without a context, brute being. Literature can help us to maintain this tension: Raymond Williams's definition of the most complete kind of novel is precisely that in which the characters and situations are seen as absolute values in themselves, the objects of a real personal concern, and simultaneously as embodying the structure of feeling of a whole society, pointing beyond themselves.[1] But these aren't of course separate aspects of the people or events, any more than for us as christians the relatedness of a man or object to the redemptive pattern can be divided off from his selfhood. And so the awareness of the relatedness of all men to the same principle gives the basic sense of equality: they are built into the same life and moved by the same spirit; or, if they reject Christ, they are related to the pattern in that way, through rejection. Men are themselves, yet related—since they are related to the same life they have a deep equality—, and therefore when we respond to them as beings-in-themselves we find our relationship to them is, through Christ, one of equality of being.

But this also presupposes a radically different sense of value. All things are equal in Christ, all derive their value from the Christ-life they show forth; and this means a quite new definition of value, because previously it was thought that things had some sort of absolute intrinsic values which could be carefully graded and compared. *Forgiveness* means cutting across this logical structure of values, a refusal to return in proportion to what is received; it is a gratuitous im-

[1] See Raymond Williams, *The Long Revolution*, London 1961.

balancing of value, a free and irrational bestowal of love in a place where objectively it is undeserved. In other words, it is the act of forgiveness which defines the Christian sense of value: we don't as Christians weigh a thing or person to see whether it intrinsically merits our love—we make the thing or person valuable by loving it: its value grows in the human response. We love people because of the Christ-life which comprehends all creation in equality and cancels out the old structure of values, we give love freely and unilaterally without calculating returns. And this again is of course part of the meaning of spontaneity, part of our freedom from law and fixed categories, fixed values. The Christian act of love is thus a human act in a particular sense, in that it is a celebration of the power and value of human energy, even when by older standards the energy is fruitless. The Christian still struggles to create and transfigure in the face of apathy and breakdown; like Thom Gunn's existentialist ton-up boys, he believes that he is always nearer by not standing still.

This idea of a revolutionised sense of value seems to me crucial for an understanding of the nature of Christian action, and ultimately of a Christian society. It forms the subject of some of the earliest Christian poetry we have, the work of the fourteenth-century poet who wrote *Sir Gawain and the Green Knight* and *Pearl*. In the first poem, Sir Gawain engages in a duel with the

Green Knight, who at one level is a Christ-figure, contracting to return blow for blow with him. What Gawain doesn't realise is that the whole idea of duelling with Christ, of giving satisfaction in proportion to what is received, is a survival of the older cyclic order which is there in the rhythms of the poem, but which Christ has broken—which the Green Knight breaks when he withholds the axe an inch from Gawain's neck in a gratuitous gesture of forgiveness. Gawain, thinking the Green Knight has merely missed his aim, leaps triumphantly to his feet and cries quits; he cannot make the imaginative breakthrough to the new ethic, he cannot think himself outside the outmoded logic by which he works. In *Pearl*, a man sees in a vision of heaven his small daughter, who has recently died, crowned as a queen, and complains bitterly that she, an innocent, should so effortlessly gain honours for which he himself has to work and sweat. He cannot see that this human system of values no longer functions; and the point is driven home by a re-telling of the parable of the labourers in the vineyard, where Christ consciously confuses received valuations, playing havoc with the wage-contract and throwing emphasis on to disproportion, free and gratuitous expenditure.

It is this element of gratuitousness, of a lavish bestowal of life which to the medieval mind was symbolised by a profusion of jewels, which most clearly represents a new conception of energy and value. As soon as the element of forgiveness is introduced into a balanced pattern of value and meaning, the pattern crumbles, and the values and meanings have to be re-defined in relation to this new, irrational force. Forgiveness can thus be a dangerous thing, precisely because it has this gratuitous, incalculable quality; societies tend to function on different assumptions, on the ideas of fixed value and rational proportions, action and reaction. We see this in the modern cinema, where the act of forgiveness has to be done totally without context, shifting a human relationship on to a quite new level, cutting across the complexity which the film has built up: this is there especially in the final scenes of Antonioni's *L'Avventura* and Jack Clayton's *The Pumpkin Eater*, where in both cases forgiveness is felt to be a different thing, in kind, from normal social experience—it follows different rules, or no rules at all. And it is because forgiveness is a total thing, to be real forgiveness, that it is so different in quality, so gratuitous and unexpected: it gives men a wholeness which cuts through the deceits and half-lies; it can be the act of fanaticism which Chris Keller in Miller's *All My Sons* saw as essential to bring the new world into being; it cuts the circuit by ignoring all the received rules. For Golding in *Free Fall*, forgiveness is "a purer joy than geometry . . . a positive act of healing, a burst of light", and the comparison with geometry is important because forgiveness has something of the detachment of geometry from the normal functioning of things, it is something quite other.

The idea of gratuitous energy is there clearly in the gospels: if a man asks for your coat, give him your cloak as well; if he asks you to go one mile, go two. It would clearly be a mistake to see these merely as acts of mortification, because they have a much more specific and subtle quality— the quality of a pure and free giving in joyful excess of what's precisely demanded, a celebration of the gratuitous. There are, naturally, dangers in stressing this too much: men who think a lot about gratuitous action often end up by throwing strangers out of railway carriages, like the man in Gide's *Vatican Cellars*. By walking two miles instead of one we might forget that there was some precise point in going one mile only in the first place; objective reality can become something to flex one's muscles on, the provider of an endless flow of delightful opportunities for men living inside their own heads. The *acte gratuit*, as we find it in Gide and Camus, seems to me fundamentally a tragic concept, and we need to distinguish between the sterility of its desperation and the fruitfulness of its sense of energy and the human creation of value.

The celebration of the value of human energy, of its creative power, comes out more clearly in a poem by Thom Gunn called *Lerici*,[1] which is in fact anti-Christian in its attitude towards death, but from which I think we can learn a good deal:

> Shelley was drowned near here. Arms at his
> side
> He fell submissive through the waves, and he
> Was but a minor conquest of the sea.
> The darkness that he met was nurse, not bride.
>
> Others make gestures with arms open wide,
> Compressing in the moment before death
> What great expense of muscle and of breath
> They would have made if they had never died.
>
> Byron was worth the sea's pursuit: his touch
> Was masterful to water, audience
> To which he could react until an end.
> Strong swimmers, fishermen, explorers: such
> Dignify death by fruitless violence,
> Squandering all their little left to spend.

The gratuitousness here is desperate, but the Christian emphasis comes straight through. Christians dignify others by loving them fruitlessly, squandering their energies, triumphing like Byron over absurdity and negation by the celebration of life. Man creates his own values—or rather, the Christ-life in him is continually creating all anew, conferring meaning in a constantly changing pattern. What is valuable is what men assert to be valuable; this is the ordinary process

[1] Thom Gunn, *My Sad Captains*, London 1962.

of a culture—a common reselection and re-emphasising—and it is through the intensity of our common attention that meanings and values grow. We think again of Eddie Carbone and Willy Loman, whose wholeness lies in an unyielding commitment—and what is at stake isn't, immediately, the objective validity of those commitments, but the value they gain through being the chosen ways in which the men concerned define themselves. So, with Gunn's poem, the point lies in the human creation of value in a response to death, in the recklessness.

Recklessness, not recking the cost, is an integral part of Christianity, but is one of the elements which above all we seem to have lost. In Gunn's poem recklessness is creative, but it comes from a man outside community, squaring up to the infinite. When this same kind of recklessness is operative in society, it shows up as a kind of vulnerability, and it is this which from the non-Christian viewpoint is often unacceptable. One of the strong points about the old system of values, of give-and-take and action-and-reaction, is that it enables you to be defensive, it stops you from getting hurt: you dole out exactly the degree of affection or attention the situation seems to demand, and you know where you stand with people. But to accept an idea of value as lying in response independent of return is to make a unilateral move and thus to leave yourself open: you can't know that the response will be reciprocated—you have to make a venture in the dark and leave yourself vulnerable, and this is dangerous in a society still functioning on the old idea of proportional response.

But, of course, for the Christian vulnerability is essential: if we're not able to be wounded then we aren't sufficiently present to each other, and total availability will mean total vulnerability. Lawrence understood this—how, to possess new life you have to venture into the unknown, you have to lay yourself open to be wounded, as Connie Chatterley does: "She yielded with a quiver that was like death, she went all open to him. And oh, if he were not tender to her now, how cruel, for she was all open to him and helpless."[1] Connie makes herself fully vulnerable, fully a *creature*—she has simply to have faith and make herself available for the new life. The situation is full of risk: Eddie Carbone allowed himself to be fully known; he had no defences, and he was destroyed. By disturbing the balance of power, by making a unilateral move which cuts across the carefully weighed values and consequences, one can touch a deeper life, of which the possibility of being wounded or destroyed is an essential condition: to achieve wholeness you must face the risk of being broken.

The task of translating these emphases into a

[1] D. H. Lawrence, *Lady Chatterley's Lover*, London 1960, 181.

political programme is very difficult, but has to be done. What has been said about the unilateral nature of Christian action has an obvious relevance to the problem of nuclear weapons, not in the sense of replacing arguments centering on the injustice of nuclear weapons which have already been well set out by the Catholic Left,[1] but in the sense of providing a depth within these arguments. Unilateral nuclear disarmament is most meaningful, as a Christian action, when it is done with a whole sense of the necessity to break the circuit of defensiveness and see vulnerability as a condition of all achievement. It also seems clear that the conventional arguments for multilateral disarmament rest on a Cartesian error which we as Christians should be especially quick to refute. The conventional case seems to imply that action is merely a kind of implementation of something that has already happened in men's hearts: that when all men want peace they can throw their weapons away. But the Christian's conception of action is much more than this: he sees action as a creative force, and he sees the act of disarmament as creating a condition as well as resulting from one. And the idea of action as being in this sense creative is very closely connected with the ideas of spontaneity and energy we have already discussed: a man can redeem

[1] See particularly *Nuclear Weapons and Christian Conscience*, ed. Walter Stein, London 1961.

himself through action: it is in action he encounters himself.

It's important then for us to see the significance of the fact that the injunction in Matthew's gospel, to give away our cloak and walk two miles instead of one, follows the injunction to turn the other cheek. Making oneself vulnerable has a joyful recklessness about it, and free expenditure of oneself involves vulnerability. We have to understand this, not just on an individual level, but in terms of a whole society, and this transition is always difficult: Archbishop Beck's hasty reminder to the Vatican Council that turning the other cheek applied to individuals and not to societies is an exact indication of our position; and what we have here is essentially a breakdown in the idea of democracy, an inability to extend outwards from individual to society. If we see the importance of an individual encountering himself in action, then we should be able to see the same importance for a society: and the point about this particular action of nuclear disarmament is that it provides society with a total definition of its own values—it focusses all the attitudes and feelings which are operative elsewhere.

For the Christian then, as for many New Left thinkers, the nuclear issue isn't one which can be separated from our general concern with a whole society. It *is* an issue in itself, of a unique kind, but it also provides a focus for a whole context of values; and action on this issue, if it is to be deep and fully self-conscious action, has wider resonances. This is why to discuss the nuclear deadlock in terms of vulnerability and creative action and value is important, because these are the same terms we can use to attack the whole basis of a capitalist society. The definition of value we see Christianity making is a distinctly anti-capitalist one, for a capitalist society above all can only work in terms of fixed values and exact returns—it has no room for the free giving of energy and the creative joy in expenditure which we have traced. Capitalist society must always reck the cost; it has to weigh every expenditure of energy in the light of a return, and the books must always balance; there's no room in the capitalist conception of work and working relationships for that celebration of human energy which we find in the gospels or in Gunn's poem. We can go back again to William Morris, who was trying to convert something like the Christian sense of value into actuality—to build a society where the value of a commodity could be thought of in relation to the creative energy of its maker. If the spontaneous-creative life of grace is understood as the alternative to alienation, then we have immediately a theology of work and society which leads us to political action on the Left, and makes an authentically Christian contribution to the exploration of humane values which has been going on there.

We can return, finally, to the idea of this spontaneous life of grace as a unifying principle underlying what has been said. The problem, in general terms, is to channel the intensity of this life into the detail of an actual culture without compromise or abstraction; more specifically, we have to see how forgiveness and vulnerability and the value of human energy can be used, as values, to attack the fundamental assumptions of capitalist society and nuclear power-blocs. The difficulty is to find the terms which best encompass a theological and political radicalism without weakening the force of either, and whatever vocabulary does this most effectively will point the best way forward.

2

Poetry, objects, and politics

This title is meant to suggest the problem, in poetry, of the relationship between the poet and the external world or particular objects in it—between consciousness and reality, the way a poet sees things, or more subtly the way he sees himself seeing things. To call this "consciousness and reality" is slightly misleading, because it could be taken as implying that consciousness can stand outside reality, over against it, which in fact we know is not so: human consciousness is consciousness of something—it is constituted by the existence of an object. But poetry sometimes gives the illusion of a human consciousness standing outside reality in this way, of a voice separable from what it talks about, and it is this which I want to examine. I want to try and argue in particular that poetry which reduces reality—objective concrete existence—to something *merely* emblematical of an aspect of the poet's consciousness can be a dangerous kind of poetry, one involving dangerous attitudes to life in general.

A good example of this process, the process of reducing reality to a facet of the poet's consciousness, occurs in Wordsworth's poem *The Solitary Reaper*, and it is all the more significant there because it is done very insidiously. The poem opens with a stanza of quite straightforward description:

> Behold her, single in the field,
> Yon solitary Highland lass!
> Reaping and singing by herself;
> Stop here, or gently pass!
> Alone she cuts, and binds the grain,
> And sings a melancholy strain;
> O listen! for the Vale profound
> Is overflowing with the sound.

This seems real and concrete enough, quite undisturbing, a direct description of a girl in a field—except for the fact that the poet's attention is double-focussed: it is simultaneously on the girl, and, with a strange insistence, on the beholder: "Behold her... Stop here or gently pass... O listen." In fact the number of exclamation marks in the stanza makes the tone into one of almost excited exhortation—an exhortation which seems slightly in excess of the objective interest of a girl quietly cutting grain in a field. This is slightly disturbing, but it is held in check within the general ordinariness of the picture—until, in fact, the last two lines, which are surprising: "... the Vale profound / Is overflowing with the sound." This has the effect of making the whole image of the girl into something more intense and significant than we expected, although the excited tone hinted at this: the idea of the vale *overflowing* with the song of a single girl is a poetic exaggeration which shifts the perspective into something more mysterious. There's obviously something more here than meets the eye—definitely something more than a girl in a field—and we wonder what it is.

The next stanza continues the slight, subconscious confusion and mystery by appearing to be talking about one thing while in fact talking about something else:

> No Nightingale did ever chaunt
> So sweetly to reposing bands
> Of Travellers, in some shady haunt
> Among Arabian sands:
> No sweeter voice was ever heard
> In spring-time from the Cuckoo bird,
> Breaking the silence of the seas
> Among the farthest Hebrides.

This is a quite common device in poetry: the poet compares something unfavourably with something else or a number of other things, so that the formal subject of his poem is the first thing—but in fact the objects and scenes which are really engaging his and the reader's attention are those which are being apparently written off as inferior. This stanza claims to be about the girl, expanding and elaborating the idea of her sweet voice, but it is in fact a way of introducing pleasing images and objects into the poem, under the guise of contrasting them unfavourably with the girl. But it is clear that the things which really interest Wordsworth here are the nightingale and the cuckoo, because both of these comparisons are in fact much longer than their place in the poem warrants: they are disproportionate to their objective function and interest, as, in the first stanza, the poet's feeling seemed slightly disproportionate to its object. If you want to emphasise the sweetness of a voice, you don't say that it is sweeter than the voice of a nightingale which sings to bands of travellers resting in the shade in the Arabian desert: this is to make what should be just one half of a comparison, and the negative half at that, quite independent, so that it takes on an autonomous life of its own. By the time the eye comes to "Arabian sands" the mind has forgotten that all this is something the girl's voice is sweeter than, and has become involved in the desert scene for its own sake. Similarly, to say that the voice is sweeter than the voice of the cuckoo which sings among the farthest Hebrides, where it breaks the silence of the sea, is to make the comparison slightly disproportionate: again the mind gets involved with the details of the Hebrides and the cuckoo, and tends to forget about the girl.

I think that the way Wordsworth uses these

images in such an expanded way points to what I take to be the really important point about the whole poem: the fact that he is not really very interested in the girl at all, although he pretends he is. This is the secret of the disproportion in the first stanza between feeling and object—the fact that he is really interested in the process of human watching and feeling, and not primarily in the girl, who is the cause of the feeling and object of the watching.

He goes on, in the third stanza, to make this fact even clearer:

> Will no-one tell me what she sings?
> Perhaps the plaintive numbers flow
> For old, unhappy, far-off things,
> And battles long ago;
> Or is it some more humble lay,
> Familiar matter of today?
> Some natural sorrow, loss or pain,
> That has been, and may be again!

Now, much more obviously, the girl has become an abstract point of reference through which the poet can touch a number of scattered experiences: it is what she sings about, now, which interests him, not her, the singer, and not even one *particular* thing she is singing about: the fact that the girl is presumably singing in Gaelic means that he can have the delight of imagining myriad possibilities, without any actual fact: the girl's voice serves simply as a mysterious starting-point, a basis for reflections on human emotion in general, on historical themes and domestic tragedies. Listening to her, he can become involved in his own private preoccupations, indulging his subjective feelings and finding these reflected in the girl's song. Because the song is unintelligible, and therefore not any one thing in particular, he can read into it whatever he wants.

Finally, in the last stanza, he moves off:

> What'er the theme, the Maiden sung
> As if her song could have no ending;
> I saw her singing at her work,
> And o'er the sickle bending;—
> I listened till I had my fill:
> And as I mounted up the hill,
> The music in my heart I bore,
> Long after it was heard no more.

The crucial line there seems to me "I listened till I had my *fill*". It is exactly that: the poet has now had his fill of the girl, she has yielded him the pleasure he wanted, and he will now cast her off without ever having found out who she was: the thing is almost a rape. She has provided him with a point of reference for some general musing about humanity, with a number of refreshing thoughts about Scottish battles and Arabian nightingales, and now he will go on over the hill, having taken what he needs to sustain himself. And as he goes over the hill, he can hear the music even when it is physically out of ear-shot: it is the interior music which he is hearing, the *memory*. It doesn't matter who the girl was, or what precisely she was singing about, or whether she died of a heart-attack the moment she disappeared from the poet's sight: he has had the experience, has it treasured within him; he will nourish it with reflection and recollect it in tranquillity, and the objective, physical existence of the girl is as irrelevant as it has been all along, even when he was looking straight at her. She has meaning only insofar as she is within the poet's focus; when she moves out of this she ceases to exist, except in the form of what she has yielded him quite unconsciously, the music of her voice. She is not a person at all; she is grist to Wordsworth's poetic mill; she has no meaning or significance outside the context of his own feelings. She is hardly out of sight before he has begun thinking how nice the memory will be, and in a way the experience was a memory all along: the poet looks at the present with one eye on how it will look in the future as a remembered past, and this stops him from being involved in the present in any full way. He is like Trigorin in Chehov's *The Seagull*, who was so busy watching himself experiencing things so that he could write them into his novels, that he didn't really experience anything at all—he lived the present as a memory. The same condition is there in a different way in those peasants in Chehov who can't afford the luxury of appreciating the aesthetic qualities of forests because they are too involved in seeing the trees as future firewood.

Wordsworth's poem defines one, very common possibility of relationship between consciousness and reality, one which could generally be termed "Romantic". A good deal of Romanticism involves twisting objective reality to mould it to personal requirements, and disillusion comes when the poet runs up against the brute intractability of reality, and its resistance to his designs on it. Keats realises finally that the nightingale which he has set up as a focus of personal impulses will fly off to the next valley, to be heard by some other poor fool who will probably also try to wrest it into his own particular scheme of meaning. Yeats tackles reality in a similar way in the first verse of *Coole Park and Ballylee*[1]

> Under my window-ledge the waters race,
> Otters below and moor-hens on the top,
> Run for a mile undimm'd in heaven's face
> Then darkening through "dark" Raftery's "cellar" drop,
> Run underground, rise in a rocky place
> By Coole demesne, and there to finish up
> Spread to a lake and drop into a hole.
> What's water but the generated soul?

The answer to that last question could well be,

[1] I am indebted, for this general idea about Yeats, to an unpublished lecture by Dr Donald Davie.

"Well, water's something that races under window-ledges, drops into holes and spreads into lakes". Yeats spends seven lines describing an actual, geographically traced stretch of river, following its twists and turns with the stresses of the verse, and then in the final line, with one breath-taking gesture, makes an emblem out of the whole thing. He shifts quite suddenly and without warning from one level of reality to another: from real water to water as emblematical of something in man: but he does this in a way which questions the validity of describing real water at all. If water is nothing but an emblem of the soul, why bother mentioning Raftery's cellar? This attitude to reality is a common one in Yeats: later on in the same poem he sees a swan and cries, "another emblem there!" Reality is just stuff to make emblems out of, an exterior projection of human impulses, material for one's mental landscape. Objects and places which seem solid enough are suddenly turned over and shown up for the symbols and mirrors they are: a symbolist poet like Mallarmé shows what happens to the Romantic attitude at its extreme with his belief that objects and words take their significance totally from context— from the context of the poet's controlling consciousness.

It seems a pity in many ways to have to attack such a good poem as *The Solitary Reaper*, but nevertheless the kind of analysis I have made constitutes a damaging criticism if it is correct. This has naturally to be a matter of belief: it is quite possible to think that there is nothing at all wrong with converting reality totally into whatever emblems please you—points of reference for personal states of mind. In spite of this there seems to be something suspect about poems which do this, as there is something slightly suspect about the way Gray's *Elegy* talks in concrete detail most of the time about an actual churchyard and community, and then ends with a personal feeling about mortality, which makes one wonder how far what appeared disinterested generalisation about human life was in fact all along bound up with a very personal preoccupation. But with most eighteenth-century nature poetry, the step across from objective description to subjective mood is a fairly obvious and conscious one: the scene is set and described, and the emotions it reflects or generates then explored, in an almost chronological process, as though the processes of recording and feeling were quite separate in the mind. This is, of course, the opposite of the Romantic viewpoint, where the processes of looking and feeling, describing and evaluating, are seen as unified—acts of a single consciousness.

It seems to me that poetry which sets out to convert objective reality *totally* into subjective emblems—which allows objective reality significance only insofar as it provides the expression of a personal vision—is a dangerous and possibly immoral kind of poetry, as capitalism is a dangerous and immoral way of life. Capitalism, Romanticism, and philosophical idealism all resemble each other insofar as their characteristic stance towards reality is essentially imperialist: they expropriate and manipulate for their own purposes—they take what has a real life and significance of its own and absorb it into an individual version of the world, granting it significance and value only in terms of this version, robbing it of independent, autonomous life. Idealism does this with objects; Romantic and symbolist poetry with both men and objects; capitalism mostly with men, but to some extent with objects too. It can hardly be coincidence that both Romantic poetry and philosophical idealism are very closely related, culturally, to a society living a particular crisis of capitalism, but of course to explore these relations in detail is always extremely difficult. However, it is sometimes possible to see within the work of an individual poet how this kind of poetic technique is connected with a whole range of social and political attitudes, as I think it is in the work of T. S. Eliot.

Eliot's theory of the objective correlative ought to safeguard, theoretically, against the kind of clear disproportion between object and feeling which we saw in the Wordsworth poem. The theory suggests a fine adjustment between the

two, a localised fusion of reality and consciousness so that each seems to exist in terms of the
other—the object evokes a particular context of
feeling, and this consciousness sustains and links
the objects. Unfortunately, most of Eliot's poetry
seems to fall on either side of this ideal synthesis,
so that what one gets is either an object which is
insistently there, but lacking in sufficient context
of consciousness to give it meaning, or, more
commonly, a consciousness insistently present, of
which the events and objects in the poem are
merely manipulated, poised emblems. The first
kind of breakdown seems to me to occur in a
poem like *Rhapsody on a Windy Night*:

> Remark the cat which flattens itself in the
>   gutter,
> Slips out its tongue
> And devours a morsel of rancid butter.
> So the hand of the child, automatic,
> Slipped out and pocketed a toy that was run-
>   ning along the quay.
> I could see nothing behind that child's eye.
> I have seen eyes in the street
> Trying to peer through lighted shutters,
> And a crab one afternoon in a pool,
> An old crab with barnacles on his back,
> Gripped the end of a stick which I held him.

One can see the connections here, but part of the
conscious effect of the passage is to make them
sterile, mechanical: the objects are too brutally

present, as separate entities, to allow the linking consciousness to come through. But in the *Waste Land*, for instance, the reverse often happens: the feeling, the particular consciousness, is felt to be twisting people and objects to its own shape:

> . . . the evening hour that strives
> Homeward, and brings the sailor home from
> sea,
> The typist home at tea-time, clears her break-
> fast, lights
> Her stove, and lays out food in tins.
> Out of the window perilously spread
> Her drying combinations touched by the sun's
> last rays,
> On the divan are piled (at night her bed)
> Stockings, slippers, camisoles and stays . . .

It's all there, every squalid detail: Eliot doesn't miss a trick. We all know the argument by now: modern life is cluttered and sordid, full of squalid, trivial characters like the typist, with her dirty little flat and love-affair. Eliot doesn't himself have to live in a flat and eat out of tins, of course: he is an observer, looking with Tiresias from outside, detached. All one has to do is to arrange the details carefully, not forgetting the picture-postcard combinations out of the window and a subtle, cosmic contrast with the sun, and the scene speaks for itself. Eliot does this frequently in the *Waste Land*, and is extremely skilful at it: he manipulates and loads, selecting and organising his effects so that we come to accept his version of the world as a natural fact. But Eliot's version of people is in fact a highly specialised one: the Cockney women in the pub at the end of *A Game of Chess* aren't for Eliot simply particular women: they are a class, and a way of life, which politically he thinks unchanging and unchangeable: here, with a few aitches dropped, are the women of Canterbury. And so a highly selective pattern of detail is offered with the posited assurance of objective reality: a patch-work, got-up version of life is offered as the real thing, and part of the point is that the reader should forget that this is highly personal, the creation of an intensely biased individual mind, and take it as natural.

But perhaps, in making this kind of criticism of Eliot, one is merely criticising the whole process of art. Doesn't all art involve a biased and personal selectivity which is offered as reality? Yes, but this selectivity must take place within the context of a respect for reality, for what is actually there beyond oneself, beyond one's own life. Art is indeed significant organisation, but this organisation demands a responsiveness to things as they are, a willingness to go deeper than external handling and category judgements. Only then can the artist begin to organise and connect: if he doesn't go below the surface, if he is content with the easy response, his connections will merely be ways of reinforcing the caricature of reality—of making juxtaposition do the work of real, responsive analysis. If we want an alternative version of seeing to Eliot, we can turn to Lawrence, who understood the artist's need to be open to kinds of life beyond himself—life which he can explore but never exploit. (I think, incidentally, that Lawrence reveals another kind of extreme, but more of this later.) The objection to Eliot's *Waste Land* technique, then, isn't that this is a personal version: it is that it is a personal version which seems to grow, not from genuine responsiveness to how things are, but from a pre-existent consciousness which then arranges reality in corresponding patterns.

Eliot, then, is one good example, in some of his work, of the dangers of this kind of poetry. Poetry which sees objects and people as useful emblems for a personal mood, rather than as autonomous lives moving within their own patterns, can connect easily with a general kind of imperialism—one which sees men as pawns to be used. Donald Davie's comment about Pound's manipulation of imagery is worth noting here: a man who can tear a single image out of its context and make it stand glowingly alone is a man who can applaud when a dictator does the same thing with himself.

It seems then that poets should see reality as something more than projected facets of their own consciousness, and recognise in some way the independent life of things. But there is an important sense also in which it is untrue that things have independent lives and meanings apart from man, and this is where the problem becomes really difficult. For the state of seeing objects and people as quite separate from oneself, uniquely *other*, moving within their own patterns and fulfilling their private meanings, is an abnormal state—as abnormal as the state of seeing things merely as extensions of oneself. The two opposite stances are in fact closely related: just as an imperialist stance towards reality can be a symptom of a whole society, a whole mode of social life to which this approach is integral, so the feeling that things are totally self-sustaining, detached from oneself, can be part of the same society. The last response is in fact very close to what Marx meant by alienation, and there is a poem by Thom Gunn called *Waking in a newly-built House* which captures the feeling exactly:

The window, a wide pane in the bare
modern wall, is crossed by colourless
peeling trunks of the eucalyptus
recurring against raw sky colour.

It wakes me, and my eyes rest on it,
sharpening, and seeking merely all
of what can be seen, the substantial,
where the things themselves are adequate.

So I observe them, able to see
them as they are, the neutral sections
of trunk, spare, solid, lacking at once
disconnectedness and unity.

There is a tangible remoteness
of the air about me, its clean chill
ordering every room of the hill-
top house, and convoking absences.

Calmly, perception rests on the things,
and is aware of them only in
their precise definition, their fine
lack of even potential meaning.

This is a poem about objects as they are, quite
separate from the human beings who struggle to
give them meanings: the things themselves are
adequate, they lack even potential meanings.
Things in the clean air of the newly built house
do not point beyond themselves, and the poet's
most positive achievement is to resist the pressure
to link and symbolise, to see them merely as they
are. They lack disconnectedness as well as unity:
in other words he cannot even force a point, a
significance, out of their lack of coherence with
each other, as Eliot might have done. Their
"is-ness", autonomy, is not an objective correlative of a state of human consciousness; it is
simply the way things are. Gunn is not of course
regretting this inability to place meanings on

things; he is celebrating it. The achievement of a condition in which things can be seen in themselves, cleaned of the mess of human patterning, is for him a positive one. As he has said in a review in *Encounter*, "it is a humane action to attempt the rendering of a thing, person or experience in the exact terms of its existence". He makes this clear, again, in another poem called *Flying above California*:

> . . . on fogless days by the Pacific
> there is a hard cold light without break
>
> that reveals merely what is—no more
> and no less. That limiting candour,
> that accuracy of the beaches,
> is part of the ultimate richness.

For Gunn, the condition of alienation is a creative one: once one has stripped and refined reality of its human colouring, one can rest on a hard, firm bedrock of ultimate truth. But this hard, cold refining, this stripping off of accumulated meanings, can be a radically inhuman process as well. Stripping away distorting human symbolisation from the world may well be an essential process: we need to regain a sense of how things are, a respect for reality, if we are to build again—to construct our meanings on a solid basis. But for Gunn, the stripping down is not instrumental to a new understanding, but an end in itself: the ultimate richness is to know things as they are, in hard, fixed separation from oneself. As soon as the newly-built house is inhabited, soiled by human contact and use, it loses its essential purity of being; when the windowpanes stop being themselves and become things to look out of and clean and hang curtains over, reality for Gunn has been blurred. There are many objections to be brought against this idea. To begin with, once this is accepted, how can poetry be possible at all? Poetry, then, can simply be about the need to see things as they are, to resist imposing definitions—and every poem will have to repeat the theme *ad infinitum*, talking endlessly about how you cannot really say anything. Gunn's poetry shows up this deadlock: it is there in a poem like *Considering the Snail*:

> The snail pushes through a green
> night, for the grass is heavy
> with water and meets over
> the bright path he makes, where rain
> has darkened the earth's dark. He
> moves in a wood of desire,
>
> pale antlers barely stirring
> as he hunts. I cannot tell
> what power is at work, drenched there
> with purpose, knowing nothing.
> What is a snail's fury? All
> I think is that if later

> I parted the blades above
> the tunnel and saw the thin
> trail of broken white across
> litter, I would never have
> imagined the slow passion
> to that deliberate progress.

"What is a snail's fury?" All the poet can say when considering the snail is that this is some kind of life which is quite beyond him, beyond the reach and control of his meanings. He can watch its progress but know nothing about it; he is totally alienated from it, and can make poetry only out of the experience of alienation.

Gunn is very much influenced by existentialist thought, and it is probably from Sartre that he takes his sense of alienation most directly. Sartre's sense of detachment from things has been a central aspect of his earlier work, and it is this kind of intense experience of otherness, as it appears in a novel like *La Nausée*, which is generalised in his later work into the basis of a philosophical (and finally of a political) position. In *La Nausée*, the hero is physically sickened by the brute "is-ness" of things, of tree-roots and pieces of litter: they exist beyond the edges of his private consciousness, meaningless and obscenely present, part of no pattern and lacking both in inherent meanings and humanly conferred significances. Objects resist even the degree of human ordering involved in giving them names, in human language: words refuse to "stick" to the objects they are meant to describe, objects continually evade human categorisation. In *Being and Nothingness,* this sense of a paralytic breakdown between subjective consciousness and objective reality has become *le néant*—the void which intervenes between self and others, self and action. In Sartre's most recent work, this sense of the self as a subjective consciousness inserted into a world of objects is very strong, and clearly influenced by Heidegger: the self tries to pattern objects (which include other men, who are present to it as opaque and mysterious) to its own purposes, but this patterning is constantly in tension with the subjective purposes and patternings of the objects themselves. Human existence then becomes a continuing conflict between the human effort to reduce the brute "thereness" of reality to ordered significance, and the resistance of reality itself to this reduction.

For Gunn, as we have seen, this tension should not exist: any attempt to negotiate human meanings from reality is a mistake, an imposition from the outside. This has been a common feeling with some recent English poets, as Charles Tomlinson's *Farewell to Van Gogh* makes clear:

The quiet deepens. You will not persuade
One leaf of the accomplished, steady, darkening
   ing
Chestnut-tower to displace itself

With more of violence than the air supplies
When, gathering dusk, the pond brims evenly,
And we must be content with stillness.

Unhastening, daylight withdraws from us its
    shapes
Into their central calm. Stone by stone
Your rhetoric is dispersed, until the earth
Becomes once more the earth, the leaves
A sharp partition against the cooling blue

Farewell, and for your instructive frenzy
Gratitude. The world does not end tonight
And the fruit that we shall pick tomorrow
Awaits us, weighing the unstripped bough.

This, again, is a poem about the need to face the natural alienation which exists between consciousness and reality, self and nature. Dusk is a useful image of this, because it is a quite autonomous process which can neither be slowed nor hurried: it removes objects from our sight with its own rhythm, and we must be content with this. The artist's rhetoric is dispersed: the human meanings he has created from objects become redundant as the objects slide away into the darkness, and if the frenzy is instructive, it is so only because we have learnt how irrelevant it really is: dusk will go on gathering, the pond will go on brimming and the sky cooling, in spite of human effort. The world will end in its own good time, not to fit in with one of our moods.

There is a poem by Christopher Middleton, called *Pointed Boots*, on the same theme:

At three in the morning
A quietness descends on central railway sta-
    tions.

A mail-van, or an ambulance may be there;
A man in pointed boots, a Miss Carew;

A quietness keeps them apart,
The quietness that descends on central rail-
    way stations.

It is not meant for me.
It is not meant for you.

As with Eliot's early poetry, isolated objects stop the eye here, and cannot be connected: objects, including people (note that "Miss Carew", who is given the same casual status within the verse as pointed boots and vans) are simply propped around the neutral space of the railway station, and the quietness, the withdrawnness of human energy and movement, underlines the discon-nectedness. The *randomness* of objects is also insistent: an ambulance *may* be there, but there's no necessity, no rootedness: everything is chance, drift, contingency. (It is interesting, incidentally, how the image of the railway station seems exactly to focus the alienation of modern society, with its mass of people united positively in relation to a general purpose but negatively to each other; the energy and movement which never meshes into a common activity; the inertness of trains and objects contrasting with this; the irony of human disconnectedness in a place which focuses a network of humanly created communications.)

The sense of the otherness of objects in modern poetry seems in some ways to be part of a whole reaction to that imperialist stance towards reality which I began by describing, but it is itself a confused kind of response. Tomlinson seems to suggest that to perceive things as they are is the basis of a moral commitment: the title of one of his books, *Seeing is Believing*, itself suggests this. In the case of Gunn, as we have said, there is a new kind of deadlock: what do you *do* with things after you have focused them correctly, precisely? or is this itself all one can do? The extreme of this attitude occurs in the symbolist poetry of a Spanish poet like Jimenez, who has one poem which reads, simply:

Do not touch the rose: it is thus.

This kind of alienation, as I have suggested, is in its way just as much an extreme, a symptom of sickness, as imperialism. The attitude of a French symbolist poet to his own poems has a striking resemblance to Marx's description of the attitude of the worker under capitalism to the commodity he produces:

> The more the worker expends himself in work, the more powerful becomes the world of objects which he creates in face of himself, and the poorer he himself becomes in his inner life, the less he belongs to himself. It is just the same as in religion. The more of himself man attributes to God, the less he has left in himself. The worker puts his life into the object, and his life then belongs no longer to him but to the object. The greater his activity, therefore, the less he possesses . . . The alienation of the worker in his product means not only that this labour becomes an object, takes on its own existence, but that it exists outside him, independently, and alien to him, and that it stands opposed to him as an autonomous power. The life which he has given to the object sets itself against him as an alien and hostile force.[1]

The relationship which Marx describes here between worker and product has clear connections with the relationship of poetic alienation which we have been examining. For Marx, objects produced under capitalism retain a kind of aura of the alienated labour which went into making them, so that our actual way of looking at made objects in a capitalist society differs radically

[1] *Karl Marx: Early Writings*, trans. and ed. T. B. Bottomore, London 1963, 112–3.

from the way of looking at them in a genuinely socialist society. In the first case, the object is the product of a process beyond our control, and has something of the autonomous, alien, unrelated quality of this process; under socialism, the object is the product of a process responsive to human need and control, and will differ accordingly in quality.

Yeats and Gunn, then, may be taken as representing two opposed poles—ways of looking which in fact spring out of the same situation. What then is the positive way of looking at objects, between imperialism and alienation? How are we to go about looking at the world? The thing which seems most wrong with Gunn's way of looking is that it rests on a false theory of human perception, and therefore on a false theory of meaning. To Gunn, objects are somehow totally themselves, totally real, before men come to look at them and handle them: human looking is therefore not only superfluous, but possibly distorting: things are complete in themselves, without man. But this is in fact the kind of naïve realism which, as a theory, is no longer viable. Objects don't have meanings "in themselves", separate from man, any more than their meanings rest simply in man himself, as Yeats might want to say: meaning, significance, is neither totally intrinsic to the object, nor totally conferred by the human response to it. It is, in some way, a process of fusion of the two: meaning is a product of a dynamic interaction between consciousness and reality, something negotiated from the encounter of mind and world, resting neither in the mind by itself nor the world by itself, but it is that creative synthesis of the two which is the act of perception and imagination. The basis of this new sense of meaning is the realisation that the act of perception is not passive: we don't simply open our eyes on to a world already fully formed and self-sufficient, supplied with meanings which are somehow inside it: reality exists for us in terms of our consciousness of it, and perception is active, interpreting the world in the process of seeing it. We don't know how things are and then communicate about them: they are available to us only within the terms of that communication. It is possible to see from this how Gunn's sort of response to the world is really an outmoded one: we can't ever know things "in themselves"—we can know them only as they are available through perception. This is not to say that objects don't exist apart from the mind, which is idealism: it is to say that reality and consciousness can never be separated, that reality is built and shared and negotiated through our communications. Reality is thus something which in a real sense is within human control: a common human creation which can be modified as new ways of looking are learned.

The negotiating of human meaning is a process involving struggle: we have to come to learn and understand the world as it is, in the act of interpreting it, to resist imposing arbitrary designs on it, to be responsive to its reality. But as we are understanding it we are remaking it—changing it in the process of understanding, as at the same time it is remaking us: consciousness and reality are bound up in a single, dialectical interchange. Wordsworth saw this, and indeed it is this sense of unity which forms the basis of the Coleridgean theory of the imagination. For Wordsworth the universe is active: the poet,

> Even as an agent of the one great mind,
> Creates, creator and receiver both,
> Working but in alliance with the works
> Which he beholds.

For Wordsworth in the *Prelude*, the whole process of perception involves this kind of dynamic, reciprocal interchange of mind and world: the poet's mind actively confers on the mountain a new radiance, which means that the mountain works more deeply on his sensibility, and so on, in a continual interchange. In this way, the mountain is never detached from human significance, since it can only be seen humanly; and yet at the same time the process of seeing it, of learning to see it for what it is and not as some other thing, means that it is not merely an emblem. True seeing is therefore a matter of simultaneously responding to a thing's autonomy and seeing it within a human pattern, as part of that whole extension of meaning and control which constitutes human society. These are not two movements: as we learn to see a thing for what it is, open to its intelligibility, we are actively placing it in relation to ourselves and a whole reality. This synthesis, as we have seen, is being fallen away from continually: we are continually tempted to see things as brute, unconnected, or just as mirrors of ourselves. The first way of seeing is a desperate alienation which belittles and saps human control; the second is a false solipsism.

So we have to learn to see in some way things as they are, and also to see that they are part of a whole reality. In that last sentence I have used the word "see" in two different ways: to mean in the first place actual perception, in the second place understanding; the use of the same word in each case indicates that the two processes are one: we see something properly when we understand it. There is a poem by William Carlos Williams which is a description of a painting, and which shows a very interesting double-focusing—of the kind we have been describing—on things as they are, and as they are patterned and related within a human understanding: the poem is called *The Parable of the Blind*:

> This horrible but superb painting
> the parable of the blind
> without a red

in the composition shows a group
of beggars leading
each other diagonally downward

across the canvas
from one side
to stumble finally into a bog

where the picture
and the composition ends back
of which no seeing man

is represented the unshaven
features of the destitute
with their few

pitiful possessions a basin
to wash in a peasant cottage
is seen and a church spire

the faces are raised
as toward the light
there is no detail extraneous

to the composition one
follows the other stick in
hand triumphant to disaster

It seems to me that the point of this poem lies in
the sustaining of a continual, confusing inter-
play between the idea of the beggars and the
whole scene as real, and the idea that this is a
picture. This produces the effect of a subtle
irony, a constant checking and remoulding of
expectations, so that one minute we are seeing

things as they are, brutally present, and the next minute the eye is drawn, as in a painting, to seeing things in that totality of patterned relationship which gives focus and meaning. The first line begins the tension: "This horrible but superb painting"; the painting is horrible in the sense that its subject is horrible, but it is technically superb. The poem goes on:

> This horrible but superb painting,
> the parable of the blind
> without a red . . .

Who is "without a red"—the blind or the painting? The line gives no clue, and it could conceivably apply to either: the idea of blind people being "without a red" is a good image. But the next line reassures us that this is in fact a comment about the painting:

> . . . in the composition shows a group
> of beggars leading
> each other diagonally downward . . .

The mind fixes now on the fact of the beggars, but is halted slightly by that "diagonally", which hints that this is a painting, not the real thing, and thus slightly qualifies the potential menace of the beggars. The next line reinforces the fact of the painting:

> . . . across the canvas
> from one side
> to stumble finally into a bog

> where the picture and
> the composition ends . . .

Here the art and the reality are held in fusion:
the beggars are going to fall into a bog which is
located beyond the picture-frame. Next we are
allowed to concentrate on the harsh reality of
the scene and gather a sense of its destitution:

> . . . the destitute
> with their few
>
> pitiful possessions a basin
> to wash in a peasant cottage
> is seen and a church tower . . .

That "is seen" qualifies the reality by reminding
us that this is still a picture, and the next few
lines are directly about the painting as painting:

> . . . there is no detail extraneous to
> the composition . . .

The emphasis on "composition" now focuses the
individual details of basin and cottage—which
as they stood were separate and random—and
brings them together into a total significance;
the poem ends with the idea of the beggars
following each other "triumphant to disaster",
where "triumphant" is both about the foolish
arrogance of the beggars, and the triumphant
achievement of the art-work, echoing "superb"
in the first line.

Williams's poem is not about consciousness
and reality in a direct way, but we can begin to

see in it the sense of balance between things as they are and as they are related. Perhaps we can see the problem more clearly if we turn for a moment from the idea of poetry to the idea of *work*, and examine the relationship to the world implied in this idea. The most meaningful accounts of work seem to me to be those of the Christian and the Marxist, which anyway come to very much the same thing. For the Marxist, work is the extension of human control over reality— the shared and collaborative making of meanings, the transforming of nature. This is at the root of Marxist humanism, as it is at the root of Christian humanism: for the Christian, too, work is the communal gathering of all creation into the human community. Christ is drawing all things through us to himself, and we extend and make effective his kingship over all creation through our activity in the world. Previously things were brute and meaningless, insubordinate to man, but now they are given over to man in Christ: man is now the lord of creation, at the centre of all things. Man is in the world to transform it and give it meaning, but the process of creating meaning is dialectical; it involves a struggle, as we saw in Sartre, against the tendency of fallen creation to run counter to human shaping. To transform, to make creation one's own, it is necessary to be responsive to the world: to see things as real, solid, not as emblems. Both Christian and Marxist are committed to believing in the solidity of things, they are realists or nothing. Poetry is analogous to work because it, too, is a redemptive activity, an attempt to understand nature, to bring it within the human community: to understand something is to control and transform it. Poetry is one means of furthering man's kingship over creation.

This is why I think Paul Tillich is wrong when he talks about the need for Christians to be "sympathetic" to nature: "No one who has ever listened to the sounds of nature with sympathy can forget their tragic melodies ... the sighing sounds of the wind and the ever-restless, futile breaking of the waves ... the melancholy of the leaves falling in autumn, the end of the jubilant life of spring and summer ..."[1] This, I think, is to get the relationship the wrong way round, to see nature as having inherent meanings which it releases to the sensitive, sympathetic man. nature is not tragic: tragic is a human word, and a human meaning. For the Christian, unity with nature doesn't mean that man will be drawn into nature; it means that nature will be drawn into man.

So it seems that the way we look at the world, the kind of stance we take towards it, can determine our whole idea of what a man is. This is where the Marxist and Christian would disagree most strongly with D. H. Lawrence: for

[1] Paul Tillich, *The Shaking of the Foundations*, London 1962, 87.

Lawrence's stance towards other things, other lives, is too often a merely passive openness to meanings which are acknowledged as ultimately beyond human reach. This, in Lawrence, can be the basis of a genuine humanism, of a refusal to exploit—a religious reverence for the autonomy of other beings. But the reverence, and the responsiveness, is only part of the process: man is not just a passive recipient of vibrations from outside; he is an active, creative being. For the Marxist and Christian, man is not simply one being among many, open to the mystery and wonder of the world: he is the centre of creation, what Wallace Stevens called "the only maker of his world". For the Christian, the universe is Christocentric, which means that it is man-centred. The most anti-humanist conception of the relation between man and objects was probably Rilke's, when he wondered whether man existed just to say "book", "chair", "table"—to articulate the names of objects and thus verify their existence for them. In fact, it is by *naming* that man comes, not to confirm objects in a detached existence, but to bring them within his control, as Adam's naming of the beasts in Genesis is an act of kingship over them—an affirmation of himself as a linguistic, and therefore human, animal:

So out of the ground the Lord God formed every beast of the field and every bird of the air, and brought them to the man to see what

he would call them; and whatever the man
called every living creature, that was his name.
[Gn 2 : 19.]

The idea of God waiting with expectant interest
to see what man would call the beasts is important. God didn't give them names beforehand:
he gave them to man to see what he would make
of them, and man exercised his domination over
them by exercising language to describe and thus
control them—the beasts became their names, became what man made of them. Language is the
meeting-place of consciousness and reality, the
living fusion of mind and world.

I want to end with a poem by Jon Silkin from
his recent book *Nature with Man*.[1] This poem is
a real example of the kind of ideal relationship
between nature and man which we have been
describing; it is one of Silkin's series of flower
poems, which represent his attempt to explore a
new sense of relationship with nature. This
poem is called *Violet*:

The lobed petals receive
Each other's nestling shape;

We share the sun's beneficence;
frost, men, snowdrops.
Then the violet unfolds. Not an uncasing
of the corolla, each petal compliant
to the purpose of survival, obedient to that;

[1] Jon Silkin, *Nature with Man*, London 1965.

but as it feels
the sun's heat, that puberty pushes out
from its earlier self-clasping
two distinct, clenched halves. Stiffens them.
These fluttering portions that made
the bud separately elect
to be the flowers; the violet
halves itself, pushing apart
in two separate forces;
it divides up itself, it becomes two violet portions.
It is not a conformation of members,
each petal a tooth, an eye-lash.
On the other hand, the violet is torn apart.
Its increase is by dividing;
Its stiffened petals push further apart.
It adheres to its nature; it has no maturity
other than this.
It requires courage, and finds that
in this unclasping of its self-worship; two
portions
tentatively open. Going both ways
they absorb a huge circle
of violeted air, an intent
movement of embrace;
created, exposed, powerful.
The air is coloured somewhat violet.
It costs itself much.

Silkin is trying here to write nature poetry
which is not merely reading human character-

istics into non-human life, nor on the other hand merely saying that violets are violets and cannot be spoken about without damage to their essences: he is trying to find a point of balance between the two, so that what comes through powerfully is both a sense of the violet as a unique, self-developing life with its own impulses and growth, and a sense of the relation of this movement and growth to what we know about ourselves. He describes an actual violet, in close and sensuous detail, and the human significance comes through as a kind of resonance, sustaining and pointing the description but not taking over from it. The self-dividing and unfolding are human readings of experience, but manage to remain within the terms of the flower at the same time, so that there is a constant double-focusing, a sensuous knowledge of the violet in its inwardness, working within the context of a human concern. It is this kind of balance which seems to me to be the most creative one: a fusion of the specific and the general which is important for the development of both poetry and politics.

3

Sacraments,
symbolism, and society

In his book *Articulate Energy*, Donald Davie
argues that the attempt to eliminate syntax in
some modern poetry is based on a mistaken
theory of language—one which sees words as
"things", concrete objects, and a poem as an
arrangement of these objects. On this theory (the
theory of men like Pound, T. E. Hulme, Ernest
Fenollosa), syntax can weaken poetic effect by
linking the isolated things or images into an
articulated human context, making them more
abstract, part of a whole movement of thought
and feeling rather than actual, intense experiences spaced around a page. Davie sees that this
theory of language—language as a kind of series
of physical impulses—is a reaction against an
over-abstract idea of language: language merely
as a series of "counters", which "stand for" ideas.
This, we have come to see, is an inadequate
theory of language. Language is not just counters
suggesting something else—there is a sense in
which language *contains* its ideas, so that idea

and expression cannot be separated: language, in some way, shares in the reality which it expresses, because the reality, the idea, is formed and created *in* language. But the attempt to move language back to a point where this can become obvious, where the words themselves are the ideas, results in an over-concrete attitude to language, and it is this which Davie is criticising in Pound. Davie is looking for the point of balance: he rejects the "idcogram" theory of language—words as individual concrete "things", as Chinese ideograms are both word and object—but sees that language, and especially poetic language, isn't just abstract either. He suggests that the French language might be a good example of a language which always seems to work at this intermediate level, between word-as-actual-thing and word-as-counter:

> If Hofmannsthal is right in saying that French sensualises the intellectual and intellectualises the sensual, he may be saying that the tendency of language is towards words as symbols *in this sense*. Concretions are milked of their concreteness, abstractions are flushed with sense, until both sorts of words live together on a common symbolic level. Perhaps this corresponds to our intuition of what happens as we read a passage of French.[1]

Wordsworth, Davie thinks, is an example of a

[1] Donald Davie, *Articulate Energy*, London 1955, 100.

poet whose language seems to move at this level, and this seems true: Wordsworth's language is not just a series of concrete, "physical" words, or just a collection of abstract statements, but a close and subtle interpenetration of the two—one which reflects his sense of the interweaving of mind and world. The kind of poetry which Davie is suspicious of is the Gerard Manley Hopkins brand, which tends to rely on the power of words as physical impulses for its effect—language enacting its meanings to the point where the words are trying to be as rich and dense and concrete as actual things, and ask to be judged on this criterion. A critic like F. R. Leavis tends to take this criterion as a central way of evaluating poetry, using words like "physical" and "concrete" as value-terms. Davie is not saying that this is necessarily *wrong* (in one sense)—he would allow that there is a kind of poetry like this,—but he objects to this one possible use of language being raised to the status of a general criterion of judgement. When this happens, poems which use language in a less concrete way tend to be dismissed.

The root of Davie's objection to the word-as-thing theory is that it tends to downgrade life to the degree in which it upgrades language. If language is itself real and concrete, there doesn't ultimately seem much point in engaging in the world: the language can create its own reality, its own world—a reality which may in fact seem preferable to the world, in its deeper intensity and concreteness. We can stop short at the language, rather than explore the real world it is supposed to be describing; soon the language may come to make itself deliberately opaque, by using obscure or vague or invented words, so that it stops us short and actually prevents us going beyond it. In this way language can come to be about itself, cutting itself loose from the real world, creating a self-sufficient world of its own. It can try to do this by purging its words of their common meanings, using nonsense words and mysterious incantation to strip itself of everyday associations, comparing itself to music as a form of expression purely about itself, self-referential.

What I have just described is in fact the poetic theory of French symbolist poets like Mallarmé, and it is this which Davie has in mind when he discusses ideograms and counters. Symbolism reacts against a condition in which words are felt to have lost their freshness and value, in which they have become inauthentic, soiled by daily use; instead it sets up a kind of poetry which has shaken off this everyday world. A symbolist poem is thus a poem which is completely self-referential, which talks about itself; language is used, not to communicate something about the world, but as an end in itself. The poet wants us to listen to the language like we listen to music, to stop us from hearing what is being said and just hear words as things, sounds in patterns. This is why he has to use unusual or invented words, or crowd together the words into a dense texture: if he does this, we can hear the words without hearing the meanings.

There is an interesting comparison here with the sacraments. We are beginning to understand that the sacraments are a kind of language in which Christ communicates with us and we reply—a language in which he is present as the meaning is present in a word. Sacraments, like language, are not physical entities, but neither are they merely abstract signs of Christ—counters representing him. They actually contain him, share in his reality, by being symbols of him: the sacramental language, like ordinary language, operates at the peculiar level between physical reality and mere sign.[1] In the past, however, Roman Catholics have tended to make the sacramental language talk about itself in the same way that symbolist poets make their language talk about itself. We have been concerned to stress the reality of the language—the fact that the eucharist, for instance, isn't just an abstract sign reminding us of Christ but actually contains him; but, in reacting in this way against the protestant abstraction, we have tended to over-balance into symbolism—to make the sacraments opaque, self-sufficient realities, things-in-them-

[1] I am much indebted to Fr Herbert McCabe, OP, for this general parallel between sacraments and language.

selves. What we have done is to *reify* a means of communication into an end in itself: to forget that the eucharist, for instance, is Christ's self-communication *sacramentally* and therefore less than physical reality, and to make it into a physical thing-in-itself, so that we have no need to look beyond the sacramental system to the time when it will be swept away and our presence to Christ will be a physical one. As with symbolism, this has gone along very closely with a dislocation between this, self-sufficient language and the ordinary language of communication: the eucharist becomes the poem which offers an escape from the rough-spoken world.[1]

To use a form of communication as an end in itself is to turn communication against itself. When the idea of the real presence becomes over-physical, the damage done to the sacraments is parallel to the damage done to language in Lewis Carroll's nonsense-verse " 'Twas brillig, and the slithy toves . . ." Carroll's poem is really about itself, because, although it raises mysterious evocations of a world beyond itself, its language creates an opaque layer which holds the mind—makes words ends in themselves. (Concrete poetry is the contemporary form of symbolism, with its ideograms and self-adjusting word machines, its use of language as a visual and

[1] I am using the word "symbolism" here to mean the theory of "symbolist" poets like Mallarmé, not to mean symbolism in general.

spatial arrangement of physical objects.) Similarly, to believe that the eucharist is the *physical* presence of Christ is to make the means of communication into an end in itself; there is then no point in moving into any other kind of relationship with the world which is communicated.

Perhaps the most important influence on our ideas of language this century has been the work of the philosopher Ludwig Wittgenstein. Wittgenstein insisted that the life of a sign, a word, is in its use: the sign gains meaning in the context of an actual human communication; it cannot be seen as a thing-in-itself apart from this. The meaning of the word is not detachable from the use, the substance from the communication: the meaning will be present whenever the language is actually used, as Christ is really present whenever we use the language of the word of God. But it is interesting to notice that at one point Wittgenstein chooses an analogy to illustrate this fact which raises some very significant questions that he doesn't seem to be aware of:

> You say, the point isn't the word, but its meaning, and you think of the meaning as a thing of the same kind as the word, but different from the word. Here the word, there the meaning. The money, and the cow that you can buy with it. (But contrast: money, and its use.)[1]

[1] L. Wittgenstein, *Philosophical Investigations*, 1, 20.

Wittgenstein is here appealing to money as an image of language: money has no life or meaning outside its use; it gains meaning in terms of the human transactions of buying things, and is meaningless outside that whole system of human transactions which constitutes society. Money, like language, is a way of being present to others— a way, ideally, of being in community with them. It is the symbol of my work, my sharing in human society, and to give this in return for the product of someone else's work is to make a real human communication involving a presence of men to each other in a shared language of signs: to share a currency is to share a form of life.

What is wrong with Wittgenstein's analogy, however, is that he seems to think that this is so at present: that money only has life and meaning as a form of human communication. It is significant, perhaps, that he chooses a pre-industrial image of money transactions, the image of buying a cow, because he is ignoring Marx's comment on the nature of money in industrial capitalist society:

> Mill's description of money as the intermediary of exchange is an excellent conceptualisation of its nature. The nature of money is not, in the first place, that in it property is alienated, but that the mediating activity of human social action by which man's products reciprocally complete each other is

alienated and becomes the characteristic of a material thing, money, which is external to man. When man exteriorises this mediating activity he is active only as an exiled and dehumanised being; the relation between things, and human activity with them, becomes the activity of a being outside and above man. Through this alien intermediary—whereas man himself should be the intermediary between men—man sees his will, his activity and his relation to others as a power which is independent of him and of them. His slavery therefore attains its peak. That this intermediary becomes a real god is clear, since the intermediary is the real power over that which he mediates to me. *His cult becomes an end in itself.* The objects, separated from this intermediary, have lost their value. Thus they only have value in so far as they represent it, whereas it seemed originally that it only had value in so far as it represented them.[1]

Marx is pointing to the fact that money, in capitalist society, has ceased to be a transparent medium of communication between men—one within their control—but has become reified into an opaque system with a life of its own, controlling men. The intermediary, the form of communication, becomes a life in itself, external to man and felt as hostile. Money is a power

---

[1] *Marx-Engels Gesamtausgabe*, 1/3, 531 (my italics).

which assimilates and contains man's existence and activity and stands over against him, mediating his existence in terms of itself rather than in terms of human life. The means of communication between men detaches itself from them and becomes self-sufficient and self-regulating, unresponsive to actual human need, a tyrannical power dictating men's activity. Man becomes dominated by the very systems of communication he has created to control his life: the communications system—money—becomes intelligible no longer in terms of the human life it is supposed to sustain and mediate, but in terms of itself. Man is controlled and determined by his own products; those systems of communication which should make for community are turned against themselves and become a source of division.

The parallel with symbolism and sacraments should be clear. In all these cases, the language of communication is reified into a self-sufficient, self-explanatory system—takes on a life of its own and begins working within these terms rather than in terms of what it communicates. What happens to money under capitalism is what happens to language in a symbolist poem, and to the eucharist in a ceremony like benediction. In benediction, the bread, which is the sacramental language in which Christ and his church are present to each other, becomes a thing-in-itself, held up to be adored rather than used: it takes on a life of its own, outside the context of its use as a means of human communication. The fact that so many popular attitudes to the eucharist are shaped by this kind of relationship is evidence enough that sacramental theology has suffered, like poetry and society, from a false theory of communication.

The idea of language as creating an opaqueness between men instead of a transparency has been very strong in existentialist thinking: in Sartre's *La Nausée*, as we saw in Chapter 2, the hero feels that words come between himself and objects—that they are a source of inauthenticity, preventing him from seeing the world properly. Language can be a similar source of inauthenticity between men, as Pinter's plays demonstrate: the means of human communication, language, is turned against itself, becomes a way of confusing others or concealing oneself from them.[1] The source of Sartre's attitude here, as with so much else in his work, is almost certainly Heidegger. Heidegger looks at communication in very much the same way as Wittgenstein, as a way for men to be present to each other, as subjects—communication as constitutive of human existence, not simply as an aspect of it or an instrument. We can extend what has already been said about making means of communication into ends by noticing what Heidegger has to say about poetic communication. "In poetical discourse", he says, "the communication of the

[1] See chapter 6, pp 151–4 ff below.

existential possibilities of one's state-of-mind can become an aim in itself, and this amounts to a disclosing of existence." This sounds like symbolist art-for-art's-sake, but in fact it is not; all Heidegger means here is that it is a valid human activity, part of being human, to make special communications for the sake of sharing experience rather than for any more directly functional reason: these communications are epitomised in literature. All our communications can be ways of being in community with each other, but it is a humane act and an affirmation of human community to make communications whose purpose is nothing *but* sharing life. Literature is in this sense a liturgical activity: in the liturgy, too, we make communications with each other in Christ as an act of our humanity, not for any specifically functional purpose. What is actually said in the liturgical act of communication with Christ is not "Dear Lord, help me to be good" (which is a functional statement) but "Here I am" (which is not). The act of communication *is* the act of being mutually present to one another, self-communication, as in the sexual act. In this way, then, communication for communication's sake is part of being a man.

This can be contrasted, however, with what Heidegger has to say about what he calls "idle talk" (*Gerede*), which is much more in continuity with the ideas of alienated existence and reified communication which we have discussed already. By *Gerede* Heidegger means discourse which "serves not so much to keep Being-in-the-world open for us in an articulated understanding, as rather to close it off, and cover up the entities within-the-world". *Gerede* is idle talk in the sense of talk which slips easily from person to person and comes to lose responsive touch with the realities it expresses: it comes to take on a life of its own, detached from these realities, it does not "go back to the ground of what is talked about".[1] This kind of language is thus a source of inauthenticity: like the names of things in *La Nausée*, it interposes itself between consciousness and object, "closing off" reality, taking on a life of its own. Any creative writer will have had this experience, in writing a poem or story, of fighting off the temptation to introduce imagery or description which takes the writing one remove away from the actual experience for the sake of making the poem or story more aesthetically satisfying within its own terms. Here the form of communication, the writing, is taking over from the experience it is supposed to be mediating, becoming opaque, taking control of the subject-matter and dictating how it is to be shaped: aestheticism in art is this process of the art-work coming to operate only by its own laws,

[1] Heidegger, *Being and Time*, London 1962, 1·5, 168–170.

to become self-regulating, rather than by the laws of the experience as well. *Gerede*, for Heidegger, is a system within which realities become blurred, within which the world can be explained conveniently in falsifying terms: it is a form of what Marx called "mystification", a human language cut off from its roots in reality and therefore self-adjusting and self-justifying. (The language of US military generals can be seen as a good instance of inauthentic, mystifying discourse, *Gerede*.) By putting the word between oneself and the thing one can stop short the mind at the thing, as with the symbolist poet, fend off engagement with the actual; behind this is the truth that our seeing is controlled by our language, that language can shape (and confuse) our perception of reality.

In all these cases, then, a means of communication becomes solidified into an end. The situation described by Marx and Heidegger is one clearly recognisable in our own society: we interpret and explain reality within the versions of seeing which are dominant, absorbing reality into these and reorganising it to fit the terms of this conventional wisdom. The pieces of reality which actually threaten our regulating ideologies are either literally not *seen*, or there is a struggle to assimilate them and, in the process of assimilation, to make them harmless. George Orwell's famous comment on the use of language as mystification, by every sort of tyrannical ideology, is still worth remembering:

> Defenceless villages are bombarded from the air, the inhabitants driven out into the countryside, and cattle machine-gunned, the huts set on fire with incendiary bullets; this is called *pacification*. Millions of peasants are robbed of their farms and sent trudging along the roads with no more than they can carry: this is called *transfer of population* or *rectification of frontiers*. People are imprisoned for years without trial, or shot in the back of the neck or sent to die of scurvy in Arctic lumber camps: this is called *elimination of undesirable elements*.[1]

A society with an alienated language is an alienated society: human life, in such a society, is dictated by humanly created forms of communication—by money, language, ideology, convention. Our understanding of communication, as Christians, is leading to a deeper insight into the meaning of the liturgy: it makes sense, now, to talk of Christ as the reality which is established, in the eucharist, at the focal-point of a number of converging human communications. To talk in this way is instantly to be in touch with what is being said generally in our society about the nature of communication; and

[1] George Orwell, "Politics and the English Language", *Collected Essays*.

if we see this, we can see also that the theological effort towards recovering a new sense of the liturgy is a natural part of a general movement to a humane version of communications and community.

4

Priesthood
and paternalism

A good deal of thinking about the priest and
modern society has been about the priest rather
than about modern society. By this I mean that
we have tended to begin from the theological
end, with an enquiry into the difference a
renewed theology makes to our conception of
the priesthood, and then to go on from here to
the sociological implications: How does this new
priest with his new functions fit into modern
society? What kind of society will he create
around him? But we need to work the other
way round as well: we need to try to establish
some idea of the reality of our society, and then
see what our theological talk amounts to, in that
context. The point which needs to be made is
that there are some cases in which there is a
serious tension between what seems theologically
sound and desirable, and the possible results of
this in terms of a whole society. This is why
theological enquiry which is basically about
society—the role of the priest, for instance—

cannot afford to work on vague or superficial social ideas, on social caricatures. This is not just an abstract warning, because caricatures of our society are frighteningly easy, and it is probably not a caricature to say that this is one of the significant aspects of our society—that it makes stock judgements and category responses easy, and offers these as convincing descriptions of our experience. It is significant, for example, that the idea of our society as one of disorientating flux, of dull, apathetic masses and spiritual vacancy, is one which can be both extremely radical and highly reactionary: it can be used simultaneously to justify a new kind of society based on radical cooperation and equality, or for the restoration of a feudalist aristocracy with kindly lords and monks and colourful, starving peasants. It is obvious that we have to go beyond this kind of surface formula, if what we assert theologically is to make social and political sense.

The obviousness of this, however, has not been recognised by quite a lot of good, progressive theology. This points, I think, to a general failure in Christian social thinking, one rife throughout the last century: the paradox that all real social action is blocked or qualified by a fundamental commitment to the status quo. We can see now that it is necessary to discuss the relationships and functions within the church as part of a wider social reality—to see that the possibilities of relationship within the church are *cultural* possibilities, supplied to us by our kind of society. This is where so many neat juxtapositions of church and world break down under pressure: because what we are dealing with is not really two separate, self-sufficient realities which can then be linked, but a complex field of experience in which it is often impossible to separate elements off from each other and label them respectively as "church" and "world". The new theology prohibits this kind of distinction in many ways: it does it by seeing that Christianity is about the collapsing of the old tensions between sacred and secular, concerned ultimately with the abolition of cult and ritual and the whole paraphernalia of religion, moving towards that fully human community in Christ where religion will have become outdated; it does it also by recognising that the major way in which the layman is part of the church is the way he is part of the world: through his work and action. What we need to grasp is that the power of the liturgy as a social force, one transforming society, depends on the values and relationships we bring to it as well as on those we take from it. One could well imagine a society where the available sense of community was so slight that no liturgical community of any depth could be formed at all; one may also wonder whether such a society is not nearer than mere imagining. What we are in church depends on what we are in the world, as well as vice versa: if we do not have the language for human communication in society then we will be equally inarticulate when we come to use the language of the word of God. Equally, of course, we cannot have a fully real society without a real church; by a *real* society I mean one in touch with the reality of the world since Christ—community—and therefore a godly society. This does not of course mean a society where 51% of the population attend Sunday mass or anything of that kind, since it seems obvious that one could quite easily have a godly society which was actively hostile to religion— in fact that at times one of the marks of godliness would be precisely this hostility.

Much theological thinking to date seems to have suffered from the same faults in its attitudes towards society which literary criticism has suffered from when it has turned its hand, as it must, to social thinking. In both cases there can be a serious breakdown between meanings on a theological or literary level, and meanings in society; in both cases, too, the social thinking often tends either to stick at a fairly simple level, working in safe categories, or to make statements about man in general which are really a-social: papal encyclicals on social themes are often full of large rhetorical generalisations and human rights and duties which it is sometimes difficult to relate to any lived, complex reality. The new theology, in Britain and Europe, has been genuinely concerned about society, but its concern has often been over-selective, like the concern of some literary critics: it has tended to select those aspects of society which seem directly relevant to theological concern—the relevance of sociology and psychology, industrial problems, etc.—and largely to slide over the basic questions about the fundamental structures of the society we live in: the political questions.

What kind of society do we live in, and how does this connect with the role of the priest? I want to argue that our society has been for a long time passing through what can be called the liberal-paternalist crisis, and that the church is now undergoing the same tensions, within a much shorter period of time and therefore in a greatly intensified way. I want also to try and show that this liberal-paternalist crisis is directly relevant to discussion of the role and function of the priest, and that as a result of this, our changing ideas about the priesthood are not only theological ideas, but part of a general pattern of change in our whole society which has been redefining relationships, values, roles. Finally, I want to point out that because church relationships and roles are part of this wider reality, they can only be solved in terms of it: any attempt to abstract these relationships from the whole context within which they grow and gain meaning is dangerous. Again, this is more than an abstract warning, because many of the archetypes of progressive Christian thought reveal that kind of abstraction. They are trying to deal with matters of Christian consciousness in isolation from a whole society, and by doing this they are recognisably part of an English liberal middle-class heritage, which has always tried, with devoted and agonised care, to solve questions of human values and attitudes without recourse to the sordid realities of politics and ideology. This is a mistake, because a discussion of the role of the priest, or of the relationship between priest and laity, is ultimately a political discussion—one which raises questions of commitment to a whole version of human relations. The liberal crisis is a crisis precisely because it tries to ignore this fact, against overwhelming evidence which it has trained itself not to see.

To understand the nature of Christian roles and relationships, then, we must get some idea of what this liberal-paternalist crisis really is, and this is difficult in the first place because part of the crisis is the assurance, at times, that there isn't really one at all. It is, in other words, a crisis of consciousness which refuses to become fully self-conscious because to do so might be a kind of self-destruction. A large part of our attention and energy must therefore be directed simply to naming and identifying the crisis, discerning the actual truth of our social condition.

The effort simply to name and point has formed an important part of radical thinking and writing in Britain in recent years, and it has been motivated by an awareness that part of what is wrong with our society is that it tries, by elaborate processes which Marx called "mystification", to conceal its real nature. If we can expose this reality, we can perhaps also expose the similarly mystified reality of the Christian church.

The pattern of change in British society over the last century or so may be described as a particularly significant stage in a long change from the idea of authoritarianism as a dominant model of human relationships, to the idea of democracy. Many different and highly complex movements dovetail into this pattern, and any description must be selective and in a sense falsifying, but this general statement may perhaps be made without caricature. We ourselves are living through one particular, and in a way inevitable, stage of this growth, the stage of liberal paternalism. This could possibly be better described as a deadlock rather than a stage of growth, because although liberal paternalism seems to be a logical and perhaps essential stage of consciousness, it is also one which threatens to disrupt and betray the whole process of growth which is moving society towards full democracy. The basic fact to grasp about liberal paternalism is that it is an attempt to meet and answer radical claims and dissent without allowing its own interests to be essentially changed; this in itself suggests a kind of contradiction, a precarious and possibly shifty conjuring trick. The way this is actually effected is by the creation of a change in attitudes and consciousness within a situation which, in terms of its basic structure, remains more or less the same as ever. The progress of capitalism, for instance, has been to concede a great deal to growing and organised demands for humane responsibility, but only to a point where it can keep its essential social and economic structures unaltered. The measures restored to do this can be themselves, by an ingenious process, ways of apparently meeting democratic demands which in fact reinforce and make less vulnerable the old structures. This is part of what happens in share-spreading, for example: the capitalist can claim that capitalism has become more democratic, because controlling power in the form of shares is spread over a wider social basis; but what this really means is that capitalist consciousness is made deeper and more extensive over every level of society, and the capitalist status quo finally strengthened. It also means that real power is invested in a small controlling group, and the rest diffused thinly over an area too large to allow any one group within it significant control; it means, further, that anti-capitalist criticism is less easy and more quickly confused, as the complexity and anonymity of the new capitalism makes it more difficult to discern precisely what is going on. The whole process is one of mystification: the structures remain fundamentally untouched, and may even be operating in a purer and more concentrated way, but the offered interpretations of what is happening are coherent enough to block critical insight.

The same process—of conceding points while remaining unchanged—is happening everywhere in our society, as the old authoritarianism, with its belief in class-rule and traditional privilege, is fighting a rearguard action against the new, democratic forces. Common ownership of some industry can be tolerated as long as the private sector remains secure; comprehensive education is warmly welcomed provided public schools from which the public is excluded can carry on the traditions of class-rule; imperialist military power abroad can be relinquished willingly, provided control is maintained through more subtle, paternalistic means; full enfranchisement of the people is fine as long as the real decisions are still taken by the same few men, educated within the same traditions; culture can be widely disseminated by the BBC provided that the BBC is allowed to choose, with characteristic paternalism, what the people ought to have; democratic protest against inhuman aspects of foreign policy can be generously accommodated until it looks like succeeding, in which case the truncheons and prison-sentences are brought out.

The dominant image of our society, as Raymond Williams has pointed out in the Conclusion to his *Culture and Society*, is the ladder, and this perfectly expresses the ethos of liberal paternalism. There is a real liberalism about the ladder of opportunity: it is quite true that, apart from a few important exceptions, most areas of our society are now open to those who, during the period of authoritarianism, were rigidly excluded—the working class. We can now climb all the way up, without barriers, and a good many of us do. What is often left out of the image is the crucial fact that the climbing can only be done on the terms of those who offer the ladder: the rungs are already labelled and secure, the way up already signposted, the right moves are in all the manuals. By climbing up on these terms we are not defeating the society, we are verifying it: we are accepting the pre-labelled rungs, the pre-formed values, the ways *they* think we should live. But our own ideas about living may in fact be quite different: we may believe that solidarity is a preferable feeling to the competitive ethic of the world we are invited to climb into, and in this case we either reject the ladder, or reject the solidarity. (In practice, of course, we all make our own compromise.) Any criticism of the system can be deflected: the guardians of the values have only to point to the ever-open door of the club. And in doing so they miss the point that what one objects to is not whether the door is open or closed, but to the fact of the club itself: the fact that society should have to be interpreted as a club at all.

We can illustrate the nature of liberal paternalism in more detail by contrasting two different kinds of firm, and seeing what these have to tell us about the nature of the church. In Britain today there are firms which exemplify respectively what can be called the "old" and the "new" capitalism: I want to compare two such firms that I have had personal experience of, and try to draw some general conclusions from this. One of these firms, a soap-factory, was a good example of the "old" capitalism: relationships between labour and management were antagonistic, and all work and activity was mediated through a complex network of restrictive practices which controlled the whole life of the factory. The workers stole almost as much soap as they packed, and any young, dynamic manager would have shaken his head sadly over the whole, shabby set-up. The other firm, a chain-store, was a shining example of the "new", American capitalism: large charts in primary colours on the walls showed the workers how they were doing in comparison with rival stores, everyone was on christian-name terms and ate together in the same, streamlined canteen with pop-art on the walls. When the workers went on a coach-trip to the seaside, the coach on the way back to the store was taken past the firm's branch in every town *en route*, and the personnel manager gave everyone a brief run-down on the branch while they all craned eagerly out of the windows to see how their comrades' window-dressing compared to their own. The image behind the firm was that of the family: a significant image, of course, because the intimacy of a family operates within a structure of paternalist authority unquestionable in its naturalness. The only hostility I ever saw all the time I worked in this store was between two warehousemen, when one objected to the other referring to the company chairman without using his title.

One way of putting the question is perhaps to ask which of these two firms is the more godless, and it seems to me unquestionably that the answer is the second one. I think one has to say this, because the evident phoniness of the set-up of this second firm blocks growth towards full democratic relationship much more deeply than the open hostility of the first factory, precisely because, like all liberal paternalism, it tries to remove the possibility of actually imagining any more humane and satisfactory relationship and structure than that which exists already. Its purpose is to create a context within which the demand for community and significant fulfilment in work can be satisfied just enough to allow the basic structures of capitalism to continue unchecked—and, of course, much more efficiently than in the first firm. The process is self-regulating: the worker-employer relationship, one dependent on actual inequality, is taken and explained in terms of family relationship, and fed to the worker through a variety of techniques; the worker then interiorises the relationship and ratifies it by acting according to it: the chairman's title becomes as dear to him as it is, presumably, to the chairman himself. Within this context, any suggestion of making a move which would make for democratic equality in *fact* and not just in attitude—giving a large degree of actual economic and policy-making control to the workers, for instance—would be interpreted as an attempt from outside the system to upset the close family relationship, and all dissent is thus effectively emasculated. The open antagonism of the soap-factory, on the other hand, is creative as well as destructive: it lays bare the real situation, without liberal mystification, and from this can grow an advance in democratic and common responsibility which would be a matter of fact, of real power and decision; out of the negative consciousness, as the history of the British working-class movement has shown, can come a positive community. Beside both these inadequate images of factories we can in fact set a third image: that of a factory built and operating on the basis of cooperative equality, where important decisions can be taken in common by the full democratic process—where men are their own managers, achieving that degree of control over their own lives which for a Christian must be absolute. This image is not, in fact, simply a dream: experiments in workers'-control factories of this kind have been tried, and have actually succeeded, in some societies, mainly in countries we have been successfully trained to think of as godless.

It seems that one of the things Christianity is about is the achievement of full and free selfhood, and that paternalism of any kind is one of the ways of life it condemns most harshly. The old law, with its severe paternalism, has given way to the new, dangerous era of open freedom, where men's lives are significant precisely because suicide is always possible, where existence is significant precisely to the degree that it is precarious: the kind parent who hid the knives in case we cut ourselves is thankfully no longer around. This is the truth which even those who in the nineteenth century had the deepest insight into distorted social relationships, could not often grasp. When the pressures of a society in which all men felt themselves to be orphans were full on, the strength to resist the temptation to run into the arms of the nearest fatherfigure was often beyond reach. Often Dickens could not break through paternalism to a more equal relationship, but his search for an adequate father-image is qualified by an inward understanding of evil forms of paternalism. In *Dombey and Son*, the paternalism of Dombey is identified as a source of corruption: here, in the context of a capitalism which is still centred on the family-firm, the human disruption of capitalism can be explored in terms of a personal paternalism. Dombey's action in sending Rob Biler to a charity school, condemning him to wear a ridiculous uniform, is of a piece with his education of his son Paul into a similar paternalism. When Walter Gay applies to Dombey for money, Dombey takes the opportunity of training his son in his responsibilities:

"Paul, come here!"

The child obeyed: and Mr Dombey took him on his knee.

"If you had money now—" said Mr Dombey. "Look at me!"

Paul, whose eyes had wandered to his sister, and to Walter, looked his father full in the face.

"If you had money now," said Mr Dombey, "as much money as young Gay has talked about; what would you do?"

"Give it to his old uncle", returned Paul.

"Lend it to his old uncle, eh?" retorted Mr Dombey. "Well! When you are old enough, you know, you will share my money, and we will use it together".

"Dombey and Son", interrupted Paul, who had been tutored early in the phrase.

"Dombey and Son", repeated his father. "Would you like to begin to be Dombey and Son, now, and lend this money to young Gay's uncle?"

"Oh, if you please, Papa!" said Paul: "and so would Florence."

'Girls", said Mr Dombey, "have nothing to do with Dombey and Son. Would *you* like it?"

"Yes, Papa, yes!"

"Then you shall do it", returned his father. "And you see, Paul", he added, dropping his voice, "how powerful money is, and how anxious people are to get it. Young Gay comes all this way to beg for money, and you, who are so grand and great, are going to let him have it, as a great favour and obligation."

Paul is in an impossible situation: he detects, and flinches at, the exploitation going on before his eyes, but must accept it if he is to have the happiness of seeing Walter get his money. The point of the paternalist ethic is to make itself invulnerable in exactly this way: to exploit genuine human feelings for its own ends in a way which makes the denial of the ends entail an impossible denial of the feelings.

The church is undergoing its own version of the liberal-paternalist crisis. When any movement for renewal starts up, there are always anxious hands available ready to catch it up and make it harmless under the plea of guidance and control; the plea may be genuine, but the damage can be severe. The hands are there, hovering, each time we are told to play down our differences in the interests of a public image; each time our common heritage as catholics is made into a blunt instrument to compel submission and compromise masquerading as prudence and loyalty. Protest and dissent is accepted, but changed in tone and emphasis so that it can blend into an only slightly modified status quo; attempts are made to rationalise and institutionalise renewal by assimilating it into a whole new set of official rules and rituals. (You *must* make the responses in English, otherwise it's a venial sin.) The problem, with church and society, is how to meet and satisfy demands from "below" without relinquishing real power, without opening the flood-gates to basic structural change. The language used, in progressive catholic circles, is significant of this: "consultation" with the laity, lay "participation" in the church. "Consultation" is the familiar paternalist word: it suggests the General-de-Gaulle-technique of bending a kindly ear without any ultimate necessity to accept the opinions of those consulted; it suggests, more deeply, that the policy-making remains in traditional hands, but the policy-makers are now more willing to listen to constructive proposals from outside. This is also what "participation" can suggest: sharing in processes which remain ultimately the monopoly of others. The liberal paternalism is mystifying and self-justifying: the laity, delighted at having been consulted about how to conduct their sexual lives or how their money should be spent, forget to question the whole procedure and go away happy, without in the least suspecting that there is something a little odd in being consulted about things which are one's own business in the first place.

The whole history of English catholicism has conspired to make the present situation one of paternalism. A church which has for centuries built and consolidated its idea of itself around the fact of an uneducated laity is suddenly faced with an emerging and powerful catholic middle class, demanding its rights. This means that the church is being driven to a radical redefinition of itself; but at the moment the deadlock of liberal paternalism is holding fast, because the long tradition of conformity which characterises the English middle class just has the edge over their liberal dissent. The traditional sources of authority, by playing on the deep psychological pressures towards conformity common to any cultural sub-group like the church, can try to hold the situation in balance, guiding and shaping protest into channels which leave the basic structural realities intact. The middle-class protest has all the traditional liberal strengths of free, intelligent, and humane discussion, but inevitably it tends to stay within the boundaries which constitute the English middle-class ethos, and one such boundary is an incapacity for imagining revolution. This, in a situation which is pressing towards revolution, is a limiting factor. The situation is further stabilised by the fact that the catholic working class has been successfully shaped by conservative, and chiefly Irish, influences to a point where its overwhelmingly Labour vote often means very little beyond a traditional and unanalysed allegiance. As a result there is no generally available radical alternative, in this class, to middle-class liberal conformism: what genuine radicalism there is in English catholicism is largely the product of intellectuals who were either born into the working class, or are sympathetic to its political traditions.

The situation, then, is in a real sense one of deadlock, although radicalism is growing in strength; and the deadlock is one characteristic of liberal paternalism, a deadlock of mystification and self-justifying, circular attitudes. We are all familiar in different ways with this circularity of argument well illustrated by the comment, made recently by a priest, that if women priests were permissible, the church would not have refrained from ordaining them for so long. If Negroes were human beings we wouldn't beat them up as much as we do. The church has quite frequently used this device of arguments which really appeal to themselves for justification, and this symbolises the paternalist deadlock: the effort is to make it impossible to conceptualise possibilities outside this enclosed network.

What, then, is the relevance of this talk of liberal paternalism to the priesthood? It seems to be this: that in our changing ideas of the nature of the priesthood, we have been going through a particular form of the general process we have sketched from authoritarianism, through liberal paternalism, to full democracy. The old images of the priest will clearly no longer do: the roaring old tyrant in the pulpit, working off his private kinks on a captive audience, is still very much with us, but it seems now that history is against him. There are still catholics in Britain who believe that you get a kind of spiritual electric shock if you touch a priest's collar in anger, but our own anger that whole classes of people should ever have been fooled and gulled like this is tempered by the fact that we have come a long way, in a very short period of time. The change can best be seen within the contour of an individual life: those of us who were brought up as catholics have only to contrast what we are able to think and feel now, with what we learnt as children. These years haven't of course simply disappeared: they have left their heritage of instinctive responses and ingrained habits of feeling in us all. But generally we have come a long way, although what I want to suggest with regard to the priesthood is that some of us have not come quite far enough. If the old images of the priest as local witch-doctor have to be rejected, so, I think, do some of the new images of the priest as local psychiatrist. It may now be obvious why we have spent so long discussing the nature of liberal paternalism, because some of the new images of the priest seem to spring precisely from his transient stage of growth, and to be ways of freezing the growth in the same way that a liberal-paternalist firm freezes the growth towards full democracy. The kind of image which is commonly offered to replace the outdated authoritarian models is that of the priest as the man coordinating and guiding the social and spiritual activity of a dynamic parish community, a man genuinely committed to the creation of community and responsibility among Christians, a focal-point of social and moral welfare, which he can foster with the aid of sociological and psychological training, industrial experience, and so on. I think this image may have to be decisively rejected, and this is the main point of the discussion so far.

First of all it is necessary to question the basic structure of the parish, and thus to question much in this particular conception of the priest. The progressive attitude towards the parish is to renew it, to make it a living community, and this on any account is a preferable attitude to the conservative who wants it to remain as it is. But it is perhaps a less creative attitude than the radical position, which is that the trouble is not basically that parishes aren't alive, but that they are the wrong kind of structure. (The same argument applies to catholic education: the progressive wants to make good, liberal catholic schools, the radical tends to believe that the existence of catholic schools as a separate educational structure is itself the root of the problem.) It seems vital that Christian energies should *not* be directed towards creating a network of Christian welfare states called parishes within society, but should work alongside and within the general social movement towards a good society. The parish is in the world, but in the world in a different sense from the way in which a liturgical community centred on schools and factories and streets and offices is in the world. This kind of argument has been developed at length elsewhere: what I want to emphasise here is that, if it is accepted that the work of the church is within social structures, not in duplicated structures, then this makes our idea of the church a more flexible and spontaneous one. It means that the focuses of eucharistic community will be the focuses of natural community within society (which presumes that that kind of natural community does in fact exist in a significant form; and that, if it does not, then it must be created). Much talk of keeping the parish system has centred on the need to preserve a sense of local community; but it is also important to see how a concern with local community can actually be an obstacle to the creation of a whole community in society. Local communities depend on a measure of physical, face-to-face community which is not always available in the wider society, and this can seriously distort our whole idea of what community is; by thinking of community always in physical, immediate terms we can come to ignore the need for a more complex, less immediately tangible community, the community of a whole society, which is more abstract than a local community only in a very naïve sense of "abstract" and "concrete". What must be asserted is that the only parish is ultimately the whole society: it is here that our sense of community must be gathered and focused. The sense of this whole community will then of course be mediated to us in different and secondary ways: through our work groups, through the local geographical community, and so on. It seems vital, for instance, that the sense of community between groups should be preserved, that mass should be celebrated in the local cultural centres which we expect to be focal points of community in any good society: this can provide community between groups without generating the whole superstructure of Christian activities we associate with the parish. But it is important that the process is this way, from a general sense of the whole community, down to groups within it. What must be rejected is the fundamentally reactionary principle of "subsidiarity" (the idea that the larger group must be subordinate to the smaller) beloved of much official catholic social teaching, which is really a pre-industrial way of looking at society. We need to create a society where any *random* group could celebrate the eucharist meaningfully because their sense of community lay not in particular activities or geographical areas, but simply in the fact of belonging to the same society, and ultimately to the same species. I think it would be quite impossible to celebrate that kind of eucharist in Britain at present, although one could think of other societies where it would be much more of a real possibility. What we are looking for, in fact, is what has been called a common culture.

What effect does this have on the role of the priest? I think that the inadequate progressive idea of the parish goes along with a similarly inadequate idea about the function of the priest: the idea of making the priest a genuinely committed social and spiritual worker among Christians, and perhaps also among non-Christians. But in the context of a whole society and a whole historical movement, this could possibly be a reactionary move. For the meaning of the pattern of emerging democracy in our society is the realisation of a genuinely *common* responsibility in the fullest sense: a community of care, a community of guilt, a community of consolation. These activities, the activities of a whole people, can never be appropriated by an individual man or a class of men, no matter how well meaning, without serious damage to the whole effort towards common responsibility. Of course, within this process, at key points, we need men with specific functions and skills to sustain the growth: we need psychologists, priests, social workers, educators. But to think that the idea of common responsibility can coexist with the idea of a specific class of men who guide and nourish this activity, acting as fathers or servants or confessors or consolers, suggests merely that the full, revolutionary meaning of common responsibility has not been grasped. The confusion at the root of this is the confusion we have all been led to make between function and relationship; certain functions, certain roles and skills within society, have become traditionally associated with a whole superstructure of relationship, which is then institutionalised in terms of authority or paternalism or service. The movement towards common responsibility is the movement to return to this sense of role and skill, without its context of social inequality. We have to try to see the doctor and teacher as men with specific functions, and to resist the whole sense of superior power and position which, within the context of a particular society, these roles have come to gather. The breakthrough to seeing the doctor in the same light as the steel-worker and clerk and clothes-designer is the breakthrough to democratic equality; and it will involve a resistance to that mystique which generalises a whole status, and thus a whole pattern of inequality, out of a skill.

It does not seem enough, ultimately, for either priest or doctor to say that they don't *feel* superior to anyone else and don't want to be: this is the liberal mistake of thinking that what is involved is only a change of consciousness, whereas what is equally crucial is a change of structures. As long as priests exist as men set apart for other men to bring their problems to, whether the problems are spiritual or social or psychological, serious inequality is likely to be created, and the movement towards a common culture constantly blocked by this paternalism. What we have to do is to learn to look to each other for that kind of active help, not to one man or a caste of men; if we look to each other, that is common responsibility, if we are trained to look to one class, that is paternalism. It is no real objection to this to reply that we must anyway look to particular men, social workers and doc-tors and psychiatrists, for our welfare. We go to these men primarily because they have specific skills: the relationship then established is always controlled by this motive. But what is the priest's skill and function to be? If merely a duplicate of professional sociology and psychology, this is not only irrelevant but dangerous: it is that duplication of the wider society in our own terms which above all we must avoid. If it isn't this, is it that the priest has some special claim to be a general spiritual consoler? This has, of course, been the situation historically: the priest as the local educated man to be consulted in times of trouble. It does not seem likely that this situation can hold any longer in an educated, democratic society, where the whole meaning of democracy and equality is precisely that nobody has a monopoly of human insight by virtue of his status and training. The idea of priests as having this kind of insight is reminiscent of D. H. Lawrence's idea—in one of his own less humane moments—of an ideal model of society, in which power and promotion would be secured not by money or rank or even ability, but by something called "life-understanding", by which he meant intuitive insight into the mysteries of life: anyone with this could then shoot up the ladder to become a kind of spiritual prime minister.

It is necessary to try to make some kind of distinction between what theology tells us about the priesthood, and the whole historical accretion which this has gathered, an accretion which at points can be an active impediment to progress. The priest is president of the liturgical assembly:

this is his chief, defining function, and it involves teaching in the direct sense of actually preaching the word of God in the assembly. It seems that we may have to return to the idea of the priest's function as much less permanent and more intermittent: the priest is the man who has authority to celebrate the liturgy for the people, but the liturgy is itself intermittent, and this is part of its meaning. Why this role should involve a man wearing a black suit and being celibate and spending his time between liturgical activities in generally fostering Christian welfare seems much less obvious. We will perhaps never have a really non-paternalist church until priests (and the word "priest" may have to go because of its confusing theological implications, as well as the alternative "minister", which again suggests a special kind of general relationship) are ordinary workers with families who have this special function to preside over the liturgy in a church where the activities of teaching, welfare, and preaching are genuinely common, not the monopoly of a caste. The ideal is a self-teaching, self-caring church, as well as a self-teaching, self-caring society: teaching must be a continuous activity involving everyone, both as teacher and taught, a shared network of learning rather than a one-way action from one class to the rest.

All this clearly involves a great change in our idea of the priest, and raises serious theological issues about the nature of priest and bishop which cannot be discussed fully here. Much of what has been said here about the paternalist consciousness would seem to apply to bishops as much as priests; on the other hand the bishop has a particular kind of role which may well involve a relationship to others more general and less well defined than that of just presiding over the actual liturgical assembly. But it is clear that attempts to describe the nature of the priest in terms of his relation to the bishop—priest as a delegate bishop—have damaging, as well as useful, implications, because we can then be led to carry over into our descriptions of the priest values and relationships which are perhaps more appropriate to the role of bishop. What we need to do is to return to seeing the priest in more limited terms, as a man delegated for a specific function; and what this means, in effect, is that the priest will have no great role to play in society outside his limited and vital function. We should perhaps begin to get worried when the role becomes major: priestly societies are unlikely to be very Christian societies, as the historical evidence suggests. Perhaps it is an exaggeration to say that society is godly in inverse proportion to the number of priests around, but this makes a point: that the function of priests is in a sense to eliminate themselves so that the church can operate. I like the Bishop of Woolwich's comparison of the role of the church in society to the role of the Communist Party in

Soviet Russia: the role of the Communist Party is not so much to make card-carrying communists as to create socialist community, and similarly the role of the church is to create community and not just card-carrying Christians. The simile may be usefully extended by saying that the role of the priest, like that of the Marxist state, is to wither away so that a real, human society can come into existence: so that the era of paternalism may yield to genuine community. (This will never fully happen, of course, but at least it indicates a kind of direction.)

This re-definition of the priest's role is naturally a long-term affair, and meanwhile it is necessary that certain immediate measures should be taken to democratise the church. As long as parishes remain in their present form, full democratic control by all the people over all parish activities is vital, and the liberal-paternalist compromise of a measure of lay participation supervised by the parish priest strongly resisted. If the parish structure is to be kept, the priest must be elected by the laity, be responsible to them, and be capable of being dismissed by them. Until the church returns to its early practice of electing its ministers, no real democracy is possible.

There is one important concept relevant to the role of the priest and the nature of paternalism, and this is the idea of *service*. This idea has been commonly advanced as an ideal image of the relationship between priest and people, and church and society, but I think it needs questioning to some extent because it is another example of a theologically progressive idea which can have damaging social consequences. It can, in fact, be another aspect of liberal paternalism, a way of offering an acceptable description and interpretation of a situation which remains structurally unacceptable. Christians can perhaps learn from what Raymond Williams has to say about the idea of service, in the Conclusion to *Culture and Society*:

> A very large part of English middle-class education is devoted to the training of servants. This is much more its characteristic than a training for leadership, as the stress on conformity and on respect for authority shows. In so far as it was, by definition, the training of upper servants, it includes, of course, the instilling of that kind of confidence which will enable the upper servants to supervise and direct the lower servants. Order must be maintained there, by good management, and in this respect the function is not service but government. Yet the upper servant is not to think of his own interests. He must subordinate these to a larger good, which is called the Queen's peace, or national security, or law and order, or the public weal. This has been the charter of many thousands of devoted lives, and it is

necessary to respect it even where we cannot agree with it.

I was not trained to this ethic, and when I encountered it, in late adolescence, I had to spend a lot of time trying to understand it, through men whom I respected and who had been formed by it. The criticism I now make of it is in that kind of good faith. It seems to me inadequate because in practice it serves, at every level, to maintain and confirm the status quo. This was wrong for me because the status quo, in practice, was a denial of equity to the men and women among whom I had grown up, the lower servants, whose lives were governed by the existing distributions of property, remuneration, education and respect. The real personal unselfishness, which ratified the description as service, seemed to me to exist within a larger selfishness, which was only not seen because it was idealised as the necessary form of a civilisation, or rationalised as a natural distribution corresponding to worth, effort and intelligence. I could not share in these versions, because I thought, and still think, that the sense of injustice which the "lower servants" felt was real and justified. One cannot in conscience then become, when invited, an upper servant in an establishment one thus radically disapproves.[1]

[1] Raymond Williams, *Culture and Society*, London 1961, 315–16.

Williams goes on to describe how the idea of service breaks down because, while the upper servants have managed to identify themselves with the establishment, the lower servants have not: they cannot feel that this *is* their community, in any deep way. This seems to me crucially important for our own situation as Christians. We have to be careful that any genuine meaning that the idea of service—service as characterising a whole relationship—might have, is not confused with this use of the idea of service, by liberal paternalism, as a way of ratifying the status quo. Some of the Christian uses of the term have in fact approached this attitude: we say that the bishop or priest is now the servant, not the ruler or guider, of the people, but what this can mean in practice is often the old relationships with a new name—a name which, by mystifying people about the paternalist inequality, ensures its perpetuation. I'm not ordering you, I'm serving you—but do it, or else. We do this at the moment in politics: the way we are actually governed is of course from the top downwards, but we explain this to ourselves as from the bottom upwards, and by doing so confirm and institutionalise the situation. MPs are the servants of the public, and as long as we have the reassuring term, the description, we can put up with the reality of our common alienation from actual control over our own lives.

Having quoted Raymond Williams, whose

work has been a central influence on radical thinking in Britain, we can end by mentioning a theme which has been constant in Williams's own writing, and a major emphasis of the New Left: the theme of communication. The act of communication between men establishes a relationship which within a total society is political; in tone, assumption, stance, language, the act of communication defines a human attitude and shapes a human reality. Here the converging disciplines of literary criticism, politics, linguistic philosophy, criticism of cultural media, meet to form one of the most significant bodies of thinking in our time. What kind of communication, then, is set up in the average sermon? What are the human implications behind it, what version of relationships does it suggest? What is the nature of the language we use in the church, in sermons, prayers, hymns? Is this democratic language, language which establishes respect and equality? Or how far can we make a parallel between the attitudes of the sermon-makers towards their audiences, and the attitudes of the ad-men and controllers of media? How far, in both cases, is there an easy assumption about the "masses", who need to be chastised, goaded, bribed, mothered? What we are looking for in society is a kind of communication which will establish community between men, as in the liturgy Christ is established at the focus of a number of converging human communications.

The fullest consequence of communication is respect for equality of being: to know a man in his depth is to know that I can have no ultimate power over him, without mutual damage. If the full implications of this are seen, we can perhaps go beyond liberal paternalism to a real community.

5

The idea of culture

It is now more than two years since the "culture" debate came to a crisis in Dr Leavis's attack on Sir Charles Snow in the Richmond lecture at Cambridge, and the first thing to say about this debate is that for many people it is dead. The reasons why it is thought dead, however, seem to me significant: over the past few years there have been some important new developments in thinking about culture, and some of these can be best seen as a kind of reaction to the terms and assumptions of the Leavis-Snow debate. The reaction can be seen in the way that one of our "quality" Sunday newspapers has undergone a silent change of policy quite recently: traditionally an island of "high" culture, it has become in recent months increasingly committed to "pop" culture, and the new commitment exposes an interesting mentality which crops up all over its pages. The accent is on Youth, with a capital letter—more specifically, on the fashionable, metropolitan *bourgeois* young who need briefing about records and plays so as not to be caught napping at parties when somebody mentions Sinatra or de Sade. The linking of these two names catches the general tone: culture is fun, everybody's doing it—to be cultured is to have an interest in everything, from Kierkegaard to the Kinks. We're all democrats nowadays, and all the old stuff about standards and values sounds increasingly hollow. Culture is ordinary, a classless pursuit; it's Stratford and Luxembourg, and all the other places where people enjoy themselves.

There's a bright, self-conscious permissiveness about this new cultural emphasis which makes the Leavis-Snow debate seem something which belongs definitely to the past. Talking about culture as though it were some esoteric religious ritual available only to the few seems less and less viable: it leads to puritanical, exclusive attitudes to life in general. The new sense of cultural liberalism blends in well with the general, vague liberalism of the middle-class, metropolitan young: nobody gets intense about class or grades of culture any more, and all the real life takes place in the comfortable gap between self-parodying trades unionists and retired colonels. In this light, Leavis and Hoggart and Raymond Williams loom up as respected figures from a period whose language has come to mean less and less: the attitudes of Hoggart and Williams towards culture, it was confidently declared in a review in this particular Sunday paper, are now definitely "outmoded". For the latest fashion in culture-thinking, turn to page five.

This cultural liberalism is in many ways dangerous because basically it is naïve, in spite of its sophistication. The cultural liberal who thinks that, by talking about the native cultural vitality of Merseyside, he is detaching himself from establishment thinking, is suffering from a modish leftism which has a long social history: the mythification of the "common folk" and their culture. To talk in this way about the popular culture of Merseyside begs far too many questions. A popular culture isn't primarily a culture shared by working people, but one created by them, growing out of the texture of their lives; the Beatles culture is created largely by a complex of agents, composers, and businessmen who are part of a system which creates a culture from above, and transmits along with it the values which will ensure its reception and enjoyment. Anyone who believes that teenagers decide the top ten needs to look at a statement by Mr H. Ratcliffe of the Musicians' Union, quoted in the Pelican *Discrimination and Popular Culture*:

> Any music publisher will tell you six months ahead which tune is going to be popular. The public does not make a tune popular. Subject to certain exceptions, some flukes here and there, we know in advance what is going to be popular six months ahead, and the publishing

business makes sure a tune it wants to be popular is popular by spending enough money to make it popular.

This kind of manipulation defines a culture, and a society, which cultural liberalism of the Sunday-newspaper variety merely succeeds in obscuring. This is the kind of hard, economic fact which the metropolitan young, galloping from Albert Hall to beat cellar, have no time to stop and analyse. The critical reception of two fairly recent books on culture was significant of this: one book was *The Popular Arts*, by Stuart Hall, and the other Denys Thompson's Pelican *Discrimination and Popular Culture* referred to above. What was evident in both cases, aside from comment on the particular strengths and weaknesses of the books, was a general, cynical sense of the staleness of this sort of argument, its boring, old-fashioned brand of commitment. Both books were radical attacks on commercialist culture, the Hall book from the position of an actual political commitment, the Thompson book from a *Scrutiny* position; in the reviews the commitment was made to come through as a provincial puritanism which had to be tolerated in books about culture written by men over thirty-five. For this kind of liberal, Hoggart and Hall and Williams are the new, stuffy establishment, trying to spoil the fun by talking about politics and standards and humane values, harking back nostalgically to a dead past. Significantly, too, the older generation all look very much alike to the young: there's no essential difference made between Leavis's attitudes towards culture and Raymond Williams's, whereas in fact it is the difference between these cases which seems to me one of the most important aspects of the cultural debate today.

In the Rede Lecture at Cambridge in 1959, Sir Charles Snow outlined his idea that Western society had become dislocated into two unconnecting ways of life, the scientific and the literary, and did so with a crudity and superficiality which Dr Leavis pounced on in the Richmond Lecture of 1962. It is important to see that Leavis's attack was directed primarily at the whole tone and quality of Snow's thinking, and through this to the value of his ideas: Leavis found in Snow a windy, clichéd quality of mind which seemed to indicate a failure of inward and living understanding of what culture was. I think Leavis was right to see this, and to point to Snow's own fiction as an image of the breakdown. Snow's racy, genial, clubman's manner, his high-table asides and jokes, are certainly more than stylistic mannerisms, and the whole emphasis of Leavis's case as a literary critic has been thrown against the attitude which can take the substance of a case and ignore the expression. A man who can talk and write about culture with the slack facility which Snow revealed is merely demonstrating, to Leavis, his lack of moral insight. The centre of Leavis's attack was on Snow's failure to understand what a culture really is, what literature is: Snow's idea of literary culture is a personal one—the cultivated individual who reads a lot of novels—whereas the scientist and technologist are concerned with practical, social matters. Of course if you can combine the two this is ideal; but Snow's primary commitment seems to be, in spite of this, to what he regards as the real, social world of practice: reading novels is another sort of activity, an essentially private one.

Snow's whole attitude to culture thus has a good deal in common with the traditional utilitarian attitude. There are two kinds of life: an intense, "inward" life, and an external, social one; and the man of culture, the balanced and harmoniously cultivated individual, is the man who can combine the two, have interests and commitments in both. It is the emphasis which we can see in John Stuart Mill's attitude to culture: one turns aside, occasionally, from the business of practical living to read poetry or listen to music, and can then return, refreshed, to the cold, hard, practical world. The way the two cultures are "connected" in this scheme is by people having a foot in both, a posture which implies that they are by nature quite different things: they can be straddled but not fused.

Mill's attitude to culture, in his *Autobiography*, is worth quoting in relation to this:

I had now learnt by experience that the passive susceptibilities needed to be cultivated as well as the active capacities, and required to be nourished and enriched as well as guided. I did not, for an instant, lose sight of, or under-value, that part of the truth which I had seen before; I never turned recreant to intellectual culture, or ceased to consider the power and practice of analysis as an essential condition both of individual and of social improvement. But I thought that it had consequences which required to be corrected, by joining other kinds of cultivation with it.

This is the "two cultures" with a vengeance: Raymond Williams has pointed out how the mechanical quality of that last phrase, "joining other kinds of cultivation with it", exposes Mill's completely intellectualist approach to the problem.[1] Mill sees two cultures, one inward, private and passive (i.e., literary culture, the world of the feelings), the other active, external, scientific-intellectual; the answer is to join the two together to make what he calls later "a correct doctrine". But the answer to Mill, and to Snow, is that lived culture can never be this kind of abstract, mechanical balance. It can only be thought of like this because there is a radical misconception to begin with of what literary culture is, and it is this that Leavis isolates for

[1] In *Culture and Society*, pt. 1, ch. 3.

attack. A culture is a whole way of life, a continually growing and adjusting complex of attitudes and values and activities, and what is meant by "literary culture" isn't the private business of reading novels, but an active, living engagement in reality, nourished by a depth of belief which Leavis would call "religious", and which can be located most evidently in art and literature. Literature teaches us how to live or it does nothing, and the qualities and values it teaches can never in this sense be separated from a whole way of life, in society: to criticise a quality of feeling in a novel is ultimately to criticise a kind of society. Snow's response to the problem of the two cultures is for everyone to know simultaneously about Shakespeare and the Second Law of Thermodynamics; what is *really* meant by the healing of the two cultures is the extension into a society's common life of those values which literature nourishes, the living out in the ordinary world of politics and technology of that sense of what it is to be human which literature can give. And this, ideally, does not present itself as a movement from private to public, inward to external: a culture is that continually interacting process of attitude and activity which cancels this Cartesian division between the things of the mind and those of the body, between spirituality and productivity. The cultural explorations of New Left theorists, in particular, have exposed the futility of trying to separate art and practical living in a society where mass-communications have made us see in new, disturbing ways the interaction of economics and technology with art and literature.

It has been one of Leavis's major achievements to recognise this kind of interaction, and make the recognition part of what literary studies involves: his own work on the relation between social and literary values was an important starting-point. But Leavis himself, under the pressures of what he sees as a hostile, commercialised society, has been forced into a position which is now very different from this, and in an ironic way similar to Snow's. Leavis's whole career has been so concerned with defending the humane values which literature enacts against this hostile society, that the tension which this involves has become a built-in part of those values: necessary hostility to a particular, commercialised society comes very close to an opposition to social institution and organisation in themselves, as inherently lifeless. What is affirmed against these is the personal value, the personal relationship, which then, through the very intensity of its isolated personalism, refuses to be translated into terms of politics and technology. The attack on particular institutions and ways of feeling, as hostile to spontaneous-creative life, ends by identifying almost all political and industrial activity as hostile to this life. The answer then is the traditionally liberal belief in "personal relationships" as the response to a sick society, or the nostalgic attraction to "organic" society which existed before industrialism. The opposition to science, and the hostility to politics, go hand in hand: both are concerned with the public world, the harsh world beyond the directly personal—the world which Leavis refers to, significantly, in the Richmond lecture as "external" civilisation.

Ironically, then, Leavis and Snow are at one level quite close: both finally make a dichotomy between personal and social culture, although with different preferences. To leave the point there, however, is to be unfair to Leavis: in his case, the refusal of political interest and the stand on the immediately personal is a genuine response to a society which he has seen, essentially, as it is, impoverished and alienated; Snow's response is superficial, showing a deep conformism to the society he criticises.

It is clear why the cultural liberalism which we began by describing should have sprung up in reaction to previous ideas of culture. The emphasis on the highest values and standards, the uncompromising hostility to much contemporary experience, is felt to have dragged culture totally outside society and the common life—to have reified it into a kind of totem, passed on secretly from hand to privileged hand, polished up a bit now and then, but essentially unchanging, vigorously protected from the grubby hands of louts likely to defile it. The defensiveness, the minority possession, are again attitudes which begin as creative and end as a destructive conditioned reflex: the need to define values over against a society indifferent to them leads quickly to a negative attitude to society as such. It is natural that this sort of attitude will lead to the "anything goes" school of cultural liberalism, which for all its modishness is at least part of an attempt to return culture to ordinary living, or at least to the ordinary living of a particular class.

The problem presents itself, then, as a need to see culture as ordinary, part of the routine texture of life, and yet to retain that sense of its crucial significance in defining values which Leavis's work has always stressed. What we want to do, in fact, is to use the word "culture" both as a descriptive term, describing the whole common life of a people which makes them distinctively one society, and as a value-term, defining certain qualities of living and rejecting others. This, in fact, is very much the way in which the term "culture" is already used—to mean, anthropologically, a whole way of life with definitive common assumptions, or, in the more traditional sense, a body of intellectual and artistic work, and the processes of making and sharing in this. Raymond Williams has insisted that the term must retain both its meanings, and they must be seen as connected: the values and qualities we discern in literature will be shaped by, and will shape, a whole way of life. The two cultures are finally fused when the political and technological structures of our society are themselves ways of expressing and creating humane values. Culture is ordinary—but that means that these values must be ordinary, widely shared.

What Williams is doing, then, along with a whole group of new-left writers like Richard Hoggart and Stuart Hall, is to take the humane values which have been at the centre of Leavis's critical case, and make these into a radical critique of industrial class-society which demands political action. We have seen already that the fact of mass-communications raises a whole series of questions about the relations between economic, technical, and artistic factors: that the way of life of a society, the quality of this life, will be shaped by the content and structure of the common means of communication, and the purposes for which these are used. A concern with the structure and ownership of these communications leads naturally to an involvement with the structure of our whole society; the communications create and reflect social values, but these are values general to the society, part of the way we live and the political and economic relations we enter into. If work has ceased to be really creative, if men feel alienated from the centres of power over their own lives, if communications exist without real community, then these are properly cultural matters, both in the sense of being about a whole way of life, and in the sense of concerning quality and value. The difference, then, between Leavis and the new left becomes the difference between a man who explores the sickness of a society and pins his faith in education and personal relationship, and a viewpoint which, while fully committed to these as values, understands that no real culture can be created in Britain without radical institutional change. The English tradition of dissent from industrial capitalism which Williams explores in *Culture and Society* is one which made no division between personal and social value. The question, How am I to live, as a person? is naturally a political question. What is resisted here is the utilitarian mentality, one still common in some of our weekly periodicals: politics in the front, arts in the back.

The relevance of the idea of culture to Christians has already been well examined, most notably by Brian Wicker in his *Culture and Liturgy.*[1] If Christians are part of a community engaged in a ceaseless fight against alienation, if the whole root of our faith, as a personal response to Christ, springs from an imaginative openness to the literature of the bible, culture in both its senses is clearly an important idea for the church.

[1] Brian Wicker, *Culture and Liturgy,* London 1963.

In Christianity, Mill's division between "passive" and "active" faculties is healed, the dichotomy of fact and feeling made whole: Christian life is at once the engagement of our creative sensibility, and our practical activity in the world. For the Christian, this practical activity is only meaningful insofar as in it we are extending the possibilities of community: but to know what, at any given point in a society's development, constitutes such an extension, to know what makes for life, requires an imaginative and moral insight into our society. Moral insight is always a matter of imagination, and therefore of culture (although, of course, one would not think that it required a great deal of moral imagination for Christians to see that work on nuclear weapons or in "big business" doesn't make for life).

It is in terms of the healing of fact and feeling that we can understand the full depth of what is involved in the "two cultures" argument. In spite of the fact that Snow seems to be ill-equipped, as a mind, to expose the full implications of the problem, the fact remains that the problem exists and is a serious one, even if he himself does not seem to have grasped it at any deep level. The basic weakness in Snow's account of the problem of the two cultures is that, although he urges the centrality of the issue, and argues that its resolution is almost literally a matter of life and death, the problem itself seems to him to be one which can be fairly easily resolved, in terms of an altered educational system and a changed attitude. This is, of course, an essential emphasis, but it misses the real depth of what the dichotomy of the two cultures has to say about the nature of our society. The dichotomy cannot be healed simply by revised educational syllabuses, because the sickness runs deeper than this, and has complex historical roots which must be recognised. One of the most significant formulations of the "two cultures" problem was made by T. S. Eliot, when he said that English poetry since the early seventeenth century showed a "dissociation of sensibility" which has never been healed. Eliot took the poet John Donne, and pointed in his work to a kind of wholeness of experience which he described elsewhere as "the intellect at the tip of the senses". "To Donne", he said, "a thought was an experience: it modified his sensibility." After this period, thought and feeling became dislocated: poetry became either a substitute form of argument, or, as with Romanticism, a powerful assertion of personal feeling against what was felt as bleak scientific and philosophic thought. By the time we get to Tennyson, certain experiences are now definitely poetic and others are not, and there is a sense in which the further the poet moves away from social reality, the more poetic he becomes: poetry is a special kind of reality, with its own conventions and terms of feeling.

This is now a quite commonplace literary argument, but its total implications are highly complex, and Eliot himself admits the difficulty of exploring this theory as an historical argument. But it seems clear that what happened to poetry, in Eliot's account, is not something which happened in a literary vacuum: it reflects something significant about the development of a whole society. It is obvious, for instance, that in a society where science and philosophy claim to be the chief interpreters of reality, poetic literature will suffer a crisis of identity, and the whole place of feeling and imagination within this society will become an acute problem. It is also evident that the fact that the common life of society was during this period undergoing a profound change—a change which meant that this life was felt as harsh and mechanically ugly in many of its aspects—has something to do with the dissociation. When the common modes of living in society are felt to be impoverished, the movement towards building an alternative reality, turning from brute facts to beautiful feelings, will be strong; the Victorian utilitarian, attacking the idea of having wallpaper with horses on it (since horses are meant to be ridden), and the Pre-Raphaelite artist, with his lily and ex travagant sexual morality, are of course contemporaries, and the fact that they are contemporaries is one of the most significant things we can say about either of them. Both have lost that wholeness of fact and feeling, external reality and inward intensity, which we can call Shakespearian—they are products of an alienated society. Eliot's theory of the dissociation of sensibility, if it is really to make sense, must be seen in this kind of whole relation, as more than a literary-critical observation: a decisive shift in literary sensibility is generally a shift in a society.

By approaching the "two cultures" argument in this way, through literature, we can guard against the possibility of a facile over-simplification, and gather an idea of just how deep the split goes, and so what is required to heal this is something very far from the reformist tactics which Snow has in mind. We can examine the problem in more detail by contrasting two actual passages of literature: they are both passages from modern novels, and although neither is directly about technology, both involve technological facts. The first passage is the opening paragraph of chapter nine of Raymond Williams's novel, *Second Generation*, describing the car-factory where one of the central characters works:

In the dark bay, the raw grey shells that were being made into cars were lifted and set into lines. Climbing the steep stairs, Harold watched the latest body being lowered by the short, black arms of the mobile crane. There was a long streak of heat along its lower left side, and this caught the dusty light as it was set gently down. He overtook it and walked on under the high bulk of the dipper. Earlier bodies were already in position there, on the powerful rods that would lift and move forward, turning the bodies like animals on spits, lowering them into the first bath and then heaving them up towards the sprays, where they went out of sight. Beyond the sprays was the great oven, where the heat came down as a vibration as he walked quickly beneath it. The newly sprayed bodies were dried by this heat, without any pause in their long slow turning, and then they emerged above the turntable, at the junction with the next line.

The force of this passage seems to me to be poetic, starting with the delicacy of "raw grey shells", and going on to capture in its balance and rhythm the movement of the machinery. The sense of strength, of physical concreteness, blends into a quality of gentle precision, as the passage moves through a fine balance between the sense of the cars and machinery as actual pieces of mechanism, and, coming through this, a sense of them as alive. In the phrase "turning the bodies like animals on spits", the almost human motion and purpose of the machinery is echoed in the image of the cars themselves as living things; and the movement of light and heat, and of Harold himself, who is moving through the scene, creates a whole, closely integrated texture of life and energy. But this isn't a poeticising of the factory, an imposition of metaphor: for what has to be said simultaneously about this piece of writing is that the author has obviously been in a car-factory, and knows in close detail what goes on. The effortless familiarity with technical processes which is revealed here is not a separate aspect from the poetic creation, an impressive side-effect for the sake of credibility or "realism"; the poetry and the knowledge, the fact and the feeling, cannot be dissociated.

This can be interestingly contrasted with chapter five of Lawrence's *Women in Love*, which is titled "In the Train", and which consists almost entirely of a conversation between two of the chief characters, Gerald and Birkin. The two men also happen to be on a train at the time, which is how the chapter gets its title; I say "happen", because this best conveys the quality of the writing that makes it different from the Williams passage. The chapter opens with Birkin standing on the railway station:

> One day at this time Birkin was called to London. He was not very fixed in his abode. He had rooms in Nottingham, because his work lay chiefly in that town. But often he was in London, or in Oxford. He moved about a great deal, his life seemed uncertain, without any definite rhythm, any organic meaning.

This first paragraph, with its staccato sentences tacked onto each other carelessly, like afterthoughts, captures the main feeling. It is not just to express Birkin's own sense of a loss of meaning that this is done—the casualness, the lack of involvement in jobs and places to live, is Lawrence's too, as the chapter makes clear. The reference to Birkin's work makes us realise that we never seem to see him do any: we have to make an effort to remember what his job actually is, and even then it does not alter our conception of him. The passage goes on:

> On the platform of the railway station he saw Gerald Crich, reading a newspaper, and evidently waiting for the train. Birkin stood some distance off, among the people. It was against his instinct to approach anybody.

The vagueness of this, the supplying of bare facts, is significant: Lawrence's interest is wholly in the moral point to be made about Birkin, not in the actual context, as the lameness of that phrase "among the people" brings out. After a cursory conversation, the train comes and Gerald and Birkin get on. There is a single sentence to describe them getting on the train and sitting down, and then the rest of the chapter—about nine pages of it—is devoted to conversation between them. The conversation ends when the train pulls into London, and Birkin is spilled back into the real world:

> "I always feel doomed when the train is running into London", said Birkin. "I feel such a

despair, so hopeless, as if it were the end of the world".

It is, of course, the end of the world in a real sense for Lawrence: it is the end of .the deeply significant conversation which the pair have been having, and thus the end of the inner, intense world which for Lawrence at this point is the only one of any significance: one has then got to get out and face the external world, and this is a kind of death. The conversation on the train is completely integral to the novel, but after nine pages the fact that the two men are on a train at all becomes irrelevant. The train is merely a *setting*, with all the static, two-dimensional quality which the term implies; Lawrence isn't interested here in reality as a creative interaction between consciousness and environment, between the process of human consciousness and the process of ordinary, factual living. Gerald and Birkin could be floating on a raft in the Atlantic for all the significance the environment has to Lawrence.

What is dislocated in our culture, then, is not merely novel-reading and the second law of thermodynamics, but the whole experience of personal consciousness and feeling, and the physical, social facts of living. It is the split Coleridge described as the illusion in which "we think of ourselves as separated beings, and place nature in antithesis to mind, as object to subject, thing to thought, death to life".[1] What has to be regained is a sense of continuity between inward and external, art and politics, body and soul. Christians are already beginning to recognise the falsity of this last dualism, and the relation of this to our whole thinking about culture needs to be made. If we have advanced theologically from thinking of men as clay husks with white things fluttering around inside them, and can see Christianity instead as a revelation about men in their physical wholeness, we can try to make the same connection in politics and culture. The tradition which is traced in *Culture and Society* is one which recognised the aesthete and the utilitarian as its major enemies: the real opponents of culture are those who disrupt wholeness by seeing experience as merely private or merely public. For the Christian, the rift between public and private is collapsed in Christ: all creation is taken up into him, so that to be most inwardly myself is to be actively engaged in the world: "Prayer and ethics are the inside and outside of the same thing", as the Bishop of Woolwich has remarked. In understanding this as Christians, we are moving inevitably towards the creation of a society where this living unity of moral value and social structure, attitude and institution, can be realised.

[1] *The Friend*, section 2, essay 11.

6

Alienation
and community

Since the resurrection, the meaning of human
community has been Christ. Whenever two or
three are gathered together, in a pub or discussion group or works committee, Christ is the
ground of their communication, the living principle of their community. Christ assured us that
whenever a genuine act of human communication and thus of community took place he would
be involved in it: when we love each other we
love him. When human community is absolutely
itself, concerned with nothing but itself, it is part
of Christ; to be most purely human is to be most
Christlike, since now all human reality has been
taken up into him. In his death and resurrection
Christ penetrated to the core of that reality and
gathered it to himself, so that now he is the
creative centre of all life, the risen man in heaven
whose life we share by living the definition, which
he established and enacted, of what it is to be
human. To be less than Christ is to be less than
human: this is now the only godlessness there is,

this failure to share in the humanity of Christ. Christianity is concerned with learning how to be a man, not a god: to try to go beyond the human is to sin.

If Christ is the meaning of community, to create community now in the world is to be in touch with the reality of history in the Marxist sense of "reality", in contact with the definitive, significant direction of that history. When the Christian does good—creates community—he is progressive, bearing the meaning of history in him and enacting it, as the Marxist who builds community within capitalism is progressive, moving with history and making history move. This does not only apply to the Christian either: to be human now, with a physical body, is to be in some kind of relationship to Christ, even if it is a relationship of ignorance or hostility, and all human life is therefore towards or away from Christ: all human life shares in the Christ-reality of the universe, and to build community is to build Christ, irrespective of the conscious belief and commitment of the builder. To fall short of community is to fall short of Christ, and therefore to fail oneself, to be less than oneself: if I live with Christ's life, to lose touch with him is to lose touch with myself, it is to become a dislocated personality, a schizophrenic. To fall away from community—from Christ—is to fall apart as a person, to lose that integrity of identity which I can only have by being part of others and therefore part of Christ.

If history has a *reality* for the Christian, a significant movement, there is a sense in which for the Christian some actions can be more real than others. This is always a dangerous use of the words "real" and "reality": it is only a short step from saying that history has a kind of informing reality, as the Christian and Marxist would say, to believing that the actions and events which we experience as part of daily life are just a kind of surface, reflections of the real, "inner" life beneath. The result of this is to undermine that realist commitment to the actual which is part of being a Christian: it can lead to an unChristian concern with an inward "soul-life", a concealed spiritual reality behind physical actuality, full of stains and fluids like an invisible stomach. But this is not in fact what the Christian means by "real": an action is real when it shares in the reality of history, when it furthers human community. To destroy human community is to sin, to become unreal, negative, unhistorical. The sinner is reactionary, lagging behind the movement of history, trying to reverse what has been finally established: he is out of touch, out-moded. When a man is good he is also real, enacting that genuine definition of the human which Christ lived out, rejecting false versions of the self. This is not necessarily a matter of conscious commitment or mental attitude, as we have said: Christ did not demand that we gave drink to thirsty men because this was the next best thing to giving it to him, or because it would be a demonstration of our love for him: we act humanely because humane action is an absolute value in itself, not a test or demonstration of something else. When we give drink we need not be thinking about Christ, we need not know about him at all: we are part of him in that action merely by being committed to the action. Christ, to modify Sartre's comment about hell, is other people: he is what is established in a reciprocal act of human communication, an act of which he is at the same time the ground. To direct human activity consciously towards Christ, in the sense of conjuring up an emotional picture of him each time we do something good, is to risk destroying the whole basis of Christianity, to forget that all genuine humane action is now Christlike simply by virtue of being humane, to reduce humane action to the image of an inner love. The man who has never heard of Christ is therefore living the life of Christ when he, like the Christian, is most human: he is part of the reality of history without knowing it, just as Balzac is judged by some Marxist critics to have creatively furthered the real, dialectical movement of history in his novels in spite of his consciously *bourgeois* attitudes.

The confusion over the word "real" can be avoided to an extent by replacing it with the word "authentic". When a man is in touch with the reality of human history he is authentic, most truly and genuinely himself, living by his own life and belonging to himself, not conforming to any externally imposed code or pattern of behaviour. For the Christian, to be in touch with Christ is to live authentically, to reject all idea of conformity to external rules and laws, to fight as false any version of the self which is forced from the outside. To be born into Christ and live his life means to make myself into him in such a way that to act against him is to act against myself, to be self-divided, self-alienated. This is what it means to say that Christian life should be spontaneous: to do good for the Christian is not to conform to a law outside the self, it is to conform to the self: to do good should mean to be myself, to be authentic. This can be so because our self is taken up into Christ: Christ is the terms and language within which I live, and to step outside this language is to lose myself, to lose all articulate sense and meaning, to fall into absurdity. If Christ is the ground of my life, the centre of what it is to be me, to be good means to be myself, and grace, my sharing in Christ's life, is that spontaneous-creative life which expresses my real self most authentically—the kind of life which, in a different context, D. H. Lawrence explored in his novels.

One image of how doing good can be spontaneous and authentic can be found in the idea of marriage. In any marriage, the relationship between the two people has to consist in a mutual interiorisation of selves, a making of the other one's own, so that each thinks spontaneously and instinctively in terms of the other, in an endlessly reciprocal process. My own good, my identity, becomes united with the good of the other, so that to be authentically myself is to be in community with the other: to be out of this community is to lose personal identity, to fall apart. This ideal sort of society can only be achieved with great difficulty: the mutual interiorisation of selves involves a continual and deepening subtlety of response because it happens within a *changing* process: I interiorise the other as she is, which includes interiorising her idea of me, but my very act in doing this changes her and her idea of me, and changes my idea of myself: the whole process involves the kind of subtle and delicate readjustment which we find, for instance, in the relationships in a Henry James novel. What happens, in this community of marriage, is not just that in this way conflict is eliminated, but that both people bring each other fully into being: it is not a prudent weighing and handling of the other, but a living and changing involvement which reduces that conflict which, in a fallen world, is bound up in all human involvement. The image for this is the image of the dance: movement and growth without conflict, full self-expression for all without repression. A dance is that creation of interweaving human harmony which is achieved without any of the members having to sacrifice anything of their selfhood, without any one of them having to die to the others. The whole movement is that of an achieved and communal selfhood, a communication of bodies which allows all the bodies to be fully present and alive to each other, but within the terms of an abolition of conflict. Usually this kind of community can only be established by someone having to die, to play themselves down, as a full family community can sometimes only exist because the mother is occupied in dying every minute to all the others. In the dance, as in the Christian idea of heaven, there is full physical selfhood and community together, each is fully himself and yet fully with the others: here community can at last be achieved without any more deaths, without some people having to stand still and keep quiet.

So when a man does good now, after the resurrection, he is authentic because he is living the true definition of himself. All other definitions are now sham, false, inauthentic: to live in any other way is to be less than human, which means that the step outside community is to be less than human. Because Christians are baptised into Christ, brought to share in him and given a name and identity in him, they can only belong to themselves when they belong to him. It is interesting that this idea of authenticity, which has come to be important in Christian thinking, is also a crucial idea in social thinking, especially in the tradition of social criticism of industrial capitalism which we have inherited in Britain. The kind of criticism which social thinkers like Carlyle, Mill and Dickens made of Victorian society was often not only that it was in many ways a bad society, but that it was a *false* society, inauthentic, lacking a sound basis of life. It was a society whose culture and institutions seemed not to reflect and embody the genuine, felt life of the people, but to be out of touch with the real, living centres of the society. When Carlyle called for a return from "sham" and "speciosity" to the "eternal verities" of human life, he was calling for an authentic society—a society where human energies could be allowed to develop and real community grow. The theme of hypocrisy in the Victorian novel is part of this same concern: in a false society, a man is forced to have two selves, his authentic self and the inauthentic version which he has to present to the world, which society imposes on him. As a result, society and the social self become dislocated from the reality of life as it is lived personally: society becomes an empty shell, a self-regulating mechanism which grinds on without concern for the human life which it is meant to express and sustain. The radical appeal, in this situation, is for a society whose institutions will be in close, responsive touch with felt human life, and will mediate this without distortion. What it wants is a society where men can be spontaneously themselves, without self-concealment; the radical belief is that if men do become authentic in this way, they will find simultaneously that the meaning of living authentically is living in community. The radical appeal is therefore not merely for the release of individual energies which are restricted: in the work of Carlyle, Ruskin, Morris, D. H. Lawrence, it is a call for that authentic life of human community which industrial capitalism has destroyed.

The relation between this social thought and christian ideas becomes clear when we see the terms which each have in common. The social radical is asserting that men are only authentically themselves in community—that when community is destroyed they are alienated from their true selves, inauthentic men. The Christian believes that when a man is out of touch with Christ, in these last days after Christ's kingship has been established, he is divided against himself, self-alienated. But the way in which men are in touch with Christ, for the Christian, is by creating human community: to do this is to share in his risen life. So in fact the Christian and the social radical are saying the same thing: we belong to ourselves insofar as we belong to each other.

This is something which we in fact know as an ordinary truth, in human society. I am myself only because I come into being, as a person, through others: my idea of myself, my self-definition, is constituted by others, and "person" is a social description. At the same time I share in the creation of others as persons, I bring them into full being through relationship: human society is a continuous network of reciprocal, creative communications which establish identity. To be outside this network is to cease to be a person, to lose touch with oneself. But there are ways of being outside community other than being on a desert island. If there is a substantial lack of community in a society, the breakdown of human communication which this involves will cause a real crisis of human identity: men will be unable to feel any sense of themselves, as authentically alive, to the degree that they will lack a sense of others; they will be unable to find themselves in others, in society, in their work. We can see in the plays of someone like Harold Pinter how breakdown of communication is not an aspect of a man but a whole condition, a matter of identity. In *The Caretaker* and *The Birthday Party*, men are secretive or anxious or deeply sensitive about their names, and this is part of a situation in which they are equally confused and secretive about their jobs, their past histories and future intentions. A Pinter play is a kind of anti-dance: the detailed patterning and ritual of conversation and movement is a way of sidestepping communication, a way of avoiding being present to others: language becomes an elaborate or cryptic way of confusing other people, a protective smokescreen rather than a way of being in community with others: it becomes a source of inauthenticity, *Gerede*. Because there is little real self-disclosure, little communication, there is a sense of nothingness and absurdity: if men do not define and create each other reciprocally as persons through communication, anything seems possible, anything will go: if there is no common establishment of self one is left quite free to be what one likes, to change one's identity from town to town and moment to moment. The sense of total potentiality and freedom which this breeds is bound up with a sense of total absurdity: if everything seems equally possible, then everything seems equally absurd. Any attempt to make a positive statement about anything is highly embarrassing and requires endless padding and circumlocution:

ASTON: You could be . . . caretaker here, if you liked. . . . How do you feel about being one, then?

DAVIES: Well, I reckon . . . Well, I'd have to know . . . you know . . .

ASTON: What sort of . . .

DAVIES: Yes, what sort of . . . you know . . .
Pause

ASTON: Well, I mean . . .

DAVIES: I mean, I'd have to . . . I'd have to . . .
You see, what I mean to say . . . what
I'm getting at is . . . I mean, what sort
of jobs . . .

Pause

ASTON: Well, there's things like the stairs . . .
and the . . . the bells . . .

Both Davies and Aston are terrified of hard facts,
especially facts about work: it is significant that
Davies is a tramp and Aston has no fixed job.
Both are reluctant to pin themselves down, to
make a definite communication involving commitment to a particular definition of themselves:
within this endless evasion and euphemism, anything defined begins to seem indecent, unmen-
tionable. Behind this particular exchange is the
whole feeling, in Pinter's plays, that work is
threatening: Stanley, in *The Birthday Party*, has
no job and stays at home, terrified of the outside
world, and when he is finally taken away it is a
kind of death. But to stay at home is also, clearly,
a kind of death: the outside world, the world of
permanent, clear facts and definitions, is a
sinister force which threatens to rob men of
their identity; but those who try to shut themselves off from it simply disintegrate, lose themselves in a mesh of evasion and fantasy. The fear
of communicating verbally is closely bound up
with a fear of society, of the whole pattern of
communication constituted by social systems and

work-processes: to opt out of speech is to opt out of a job.

The behaviour of Pinter's characters is in many ways instantly recognisable as a central experience of our society. Stanley, Davies, and Aston contract out of society and work because they feel these as forces threatening to undermine their real selves, but the result of contracting out is to lose grip of themselves, to return to infancy, to live a kind of non-existence. Because they have no relationship with any other human being, they have no way of confirming their own existence: as a result they invent selves to suit the moment, falsify their past history and create fantasies, and all this becomes acceptable because they no longer have any authentic core of self to which they can conform. This experience is recognisable, because one way of describing Pinter's characters is to say that they show symptoms of schizophrenia, and schizophrenia—or experience and behaviour approaching schizophrenia—has become common enough in our society to make it plausible, in certain ways, to use the phrase "schizophrenic society" as a general description of our whole social condition.

Schizophrenics have been described, by the psychologist R. D. Laing, as people who feel "persecuted by reality itself",[1] and this confirms the aptness of talking about some of Pinter's

[1] R. D. Laing, *The Divided Self*, London 1965, 80.

characters in this way. Laing's work on schizophrenia is in fact extremely relevant to the whole theme of the authentic self, and it is interesting that he is drawing, as a psychologist, on a tradition of existentialist thought which is also significant for Christian theology. Laing describes schizophrenia as a condition in which a dislocation takes place between a man's authentic self and the self which is present as an object to others in the world: a man who is seriously unable to "embody" himself, to feel his body and his public self as part of him, is in this sense a schizophrenic. Such a man may come to feel that what is happening to him, in the public, social world, is not really happening to *him* at all: he takes cover from social reality by regarding his physical, social self as something which can be destroyed or detached without damage to his "real" self, the self inside or beyond the body. "The body is felt more as one object among other objects in the world than as the core of the individual's own being. Instead of being the core of his true self, the body is felt as the core of a false self, which a detached, disembodied, 'inner', 'true' self looks on at with tenderness, amusement or hatred as the case may be."[1] But as a result of this public/private dislocation, the inner self becomes itself unreal, split: a secondary splitting takes place within this, so that the

[1] Laing, 69.

inner self loses its integrity as a result of having lost grip on the outer self.

What Laing is describing as schizophrenia is a condition of severe self-alienation, in which spontaneous continuity between the self and its embodiment in the world breaks down. There are instead two, opposed selves: the self "inside", which is felt to be real, authentic, and the outer self which others can see and handle and talk to, which is felt to be false, a mere image or projection. Schizophrenia is thus a kind of in-authenticity: a schizophrenic is a man who cannot find himself in his actions, who can find no continuity between his own idea of himself and others' ideas of him, between his self-evaluation and the way others use and treat him. The self which is part of society, caught up in social processes and relationships, is detachable, false—it is merely a front behind which the schizophrenic tries to keep his inner self intact. But as Laing points out, "the tragic paradox is that the more the self is defended in this way, the more it is destroyed": the self finally disintegrates, not as a result of attacks from outside, but "by the devastation caused by the inner defensive manœuvres themselves". The fight to stay authentic is doomed to failure: the very effort involved in holding apart the two selves, public and private, is itself the cause of the eventual breakdown of the real self.

Laing does not treat schizophrenia as an

isolated psychological condition, but relates it to the condition of a whole society. If men are forced to retreat inside false selves, forced to detach themselves from the self which is involved in society with others, this suggests that there is something radically wrong with the kind of society they live in. It is a society in which a man cannot identify himself with his social role, with the way others see him, or with the way he is supposed to see himself; he cannot feel himself "in" himself as others see him, in the image of himself which they reflect to him. His private and public worlds are torn apart: because he cannot feel that the self which works and has relationships is really *him*, he becomes unreal, negative. The reason why this happens is closely related to the whole structure of a society which denies men full, creative selfhood and autonomy in their ordinary social roles. Men are unable to find themselves in these social roles because the roles deny and cripple their authentic selfhood, reduce them to tools or objects; when this happens a man withdraws from the role, leaving it behind him as a kind of empty husk. He carries on performing the ordinary functions of his role, but this becomes a kind of conditioned reflex from which his real self is absent. When the tension involved in this split becomes intolerable, there is a general disintegration of the self. Schizophrenia, for Laing, is thus part of the whole condition of a society where men are self-divided, alienated from themselves: it is part of a crisis of identity which in some form is common to almost all of us, and the schizophrenic is the man who focuses the tension and the breakdown most intensely.

The condition of social alienation was formu-lated and explored most fully by Karl Marx, and Laing is making creative use of Marx's ideas in his own writing about actual schizophrenic ex-perience. The idea that the experience of the worker under capitalism is one of alienation is one of Marx's most basic insights, and forms the centre of Marxist humanism: it is at this point more than any other, perhaps, that a general tradition of radical social thinking has been shaped by specifically Marxist thought. For Marx, the worker under capitalism is alienated because he can find no authentic, personal significance in his work or in the work-product; the worker is part of a system which exploits his personal creative power for ends beyond his con-trol—which demands, contradictorily, that he should expend his creative energy in a process the products of which are expropriated by another, by the capitalist, and used as part of the market system which reduces the worker to a slave. The system needs the worker to operate as a subject, personally creative and responsible, but uses him in fact as an object, draining his power for purposes alien to him, for capitalist profit. It is the workers' lack of control over the whole system, his inability to control the processes and products of his own labour, which for Marx constitutes his essential alienation; the work is not primarily for the sake of those involved in it, and therefore an equal and positively collaborative process, but an activity done chiefly for the profit of a minority, those who own and control the means of production. Under this system, the vast majority of the people are denied full selfhood, control and autonomy in their work, and, as an extension of this, in life outside work, in education and culture. They are part of an alienated society, a society unable to locate its own creativity in what it creates, robbed of the power to find its reflection in its products:

In what does this alienation of labour consist? First, that the work is *external* to the worker, that it is not a part of his nature, that consequently he does not fulfil himself in his work but denies himself, has a feeling of misery, not of well-being, does not develop freely a physical and mental energy, but is physically exhausted and mentally debased. The worker feels himself at home only during his leisure, whereas at work he feels homeless. His work is not voluntary but imposed, *forced labour*. It is not the satisfaction of a need, but only a *means* for satisfying other needs. Its alien character is clearly shown by the fact that as soon as there is no physical or other compulsion it is avoided like the plague. Finally, the alienated character of the work for the worker appears in the fact that it is not his work but work for someone else, that in work he does not belong to himself but to another person.

Just as in religion the spontaneous activity of human fantasy, of the human brain and heart, reacts independently, that is, as an alien activity of gods or devils, upon the individual, so the activity of the worker is not his spontaneous activity. It is another's activity, and a loss of his own spontaneity.[1]

Marx describes alienation here very much in the terms we have used already to describe self-division and inauthenticity: under capitalism the worker *does not belong to himself*, he suffers a breakdown of spontaneity, of what Lawrence called "spontaneous-creative life": that spontaneity which is the fluent and effortless embodiment of the real self in society, in social action. When this breaks down, when a man can no longer see his real self reflected in his products, his actions, his body, he is inauthentic, schizophrenic. For Marx, the worker is unable to synthesise his two selves: his true, creative personality, and the self which arises from his social function. For these to be at odds, to run counter to each other, is to be self-alienated. This will

[1] Karl Marx, *Economic and Philosophical Manuscripts*.

happen, Marx is saying, when a society lacks positive community; for to experience community is to experience one's authentic self and social self as fused, to experience no hiatus between the two. In this condition, I am what I am with others; in an alienated society the opposite is true—what I am with others is not what I am.

What is the significance of this for Christianity? It is interesting to notice to begin with how much the sense of not belonging to one's body has become part of what it means to be a Christian, and especially a Roman Catholic. If a man tells a non-Christian that he feels his body is a decaying, putrid shell which he feels he could peel off, the non-Christian would be likely to be alarmed and tell him to see a psychiatrist; if the man told this to one kind of Christian it is conceivable that he would be met with smiling approval. Laing recounts how one of his patients who was experiencing disembodiment was set upon and coshed, and how his reaction was: "They could only beat me up but they could not do me any real harm." This is the kind of statement which anyone brought up a Roman Catholic would feel himself instinctively agreeing with. "Of which must I take more care, my body or my soul?"—the catechism answer, predictably, is the soul. What is in fact being groped for here is the truism that, as any non-Christian would agree, there are certain extraordinary circumstances in which it is good to sacrifice physical to moral welfare; but the fact that the question is made to sound one of the same order as: Of which must I take more care, my kidney or my left foot?, is symptomatic of the degree to which Christianity has deepened and nourished a false body/soul dualism. The Christian division of body and soul, with its downgrading of the material, is a particular form of that whole rejection of the material for the "inward" which has been so much a part of our history, and which as we suggested in the previous chapter can only really be understood in the context of what kind of material society is being rejected.

The central Christian significance of Marx and Laing, however, is not concerned with this dualism, one which is anyway fast disappearing in enlightened Christian theology. Its real significance lies in its whole relation to the ideas of Christ, community, and authentic living which we began by outlining. In the work of Marx and Laing, the Christian truth that it is in Christ that we find authenticity becomes actualised in specific and revolutionary ways. We have seen already that if we substitute "human community" for "Christ", the relation is apparent: it is in genuine human community, according to Marx and Laing, that men lose their alienation and become authentically themselves. But for a Christian there is no need to substitute the terms Christ and community: Christianity is about the way community is how Christ is present in the world, the way we build him. In Christ, men are reconciled to their real selves, find their living image, live with his life. In socialism, according to Marx, men live out the real meaning of being human, find themselves truly reflected in their work, live with each others' lives.

To be out of touch with Christ-community is to be out of touch with myself, as we have seen, since this lies at the centre of my personal reality as a man. Christianity is about freedom because it is about being myself; but to be myself is to be something definite—it is not a general, limitless field of potential. If I am anything, a person, there must be limits to define me as that person and not some other, limits which I can only cross by agreeing to be less than myself, to act out of character. It is because to be myself is to live the life of a real person, Jesus Christ, that Christianity is concerned with both freedom and limitation. If I break those limits which constitute the humanity of Christ, I cease to be myself—I become unspontaneous, an actor playing an inauthentic role. To sin is therefore to undo myself, to fall into nothingness, into the kind of limitless freedom which we saw in Pinter was absurdity, bound up with an immature inability to become a person. To sin is to refuse the freedom to become a particular person for the freedom to be everything and therefore nothing. The social correlative is the vagrant, the man who dodges the responsibility of having a defining place within society, one which establishes him as a person. The vagrant and the sinner are the precise opposite of the *rebel*, who needs to be an authentic man to rebel, and establishes himself as such in the act of rebellion. To sin is to be a tramp, not a revolutionary.

We saw that Marx's protest against capitalism was that it reduced men to objects, stifling their power to become full subjects, fully themselves. In capitalist society, a small number of men are allowed full play for their subjective freedom, but only at the expense of enslaving and objectifying all the rest, as an essential condition of this freedom: the men who actually own the means of production can only continue to do so provided that they use others as objects, with meaning only in relation to their own personal projects, not in relation to themselves. In exercising his subjective freedom, a man creates and orders a field of possibility in the world, shaping the material of that world to his own ends and organising its objects in relation to his purposes; but trapped in that personal field may well be other men, other subjects, who are similarly striving to set up a personal project. These men are then enslaved, as objects, within the project of another, drained of their subjective freedom and autonomy; similarly, the men who drain them in this way are themselves involved in a continuing struggle to avoid their projects from being absorbed into and reorganised by the project of another, to whom they, too, are objects. In this condition, all men are objects to each other, potential threats to each others' autonomy of existence: each man is persecuted by all the rest, in an endlessly reciprocal process. What we are in fact describing here is essentially the condition of a capitalist society, with its dominant image of the market. In this society, one built on the enduring tension between clashing individual subjectivities, a man trapped within the project of another has formal significance only in relation to this project, which robs him of the power to experience significance in himself. The tension between the way he is used within another's project, as an object, and his own sense of personal value, as a subject, is precisely the tension we have already described as the condition of self-alienation.

The way this condition is to be resolved, theoretically, is by the elimination of the conditions in which men can be objects, tools, to each other. What is needed is a society in which all men can be equally and simultaneously *subjects*, ordering their lives with the kind of free autonomy which at present, in capitalism, is available only to a minority. One attempted answer to this situation of reciprocal enslavement and objectification has been a traditional brand of anarchism: let all men be free to be themselves without interference from others, and let society be organised so that this is possible.

But what is clearly ignored here is the fact that this response is not radical at all: it can simply be an attempt to spread to everyone the kind of freedom which under capitalism is the reserve of the few. The radical response to an alienated society is the response of *community*—community as the way of life in which all men can be simultaneously free subjects, present to each other without mutual exploitation. The radical response, therefore, is to affirm that men can be free only in genuine equal relationship, not by avoiding relationship (as with some types of individualist anarchism), or by enslaving others in order to ensure one's own, precarious freedom (as with capitalism).

But how in fact is one to achieve a society where all men can be present to each other as subjects? For the Christian, there is a prototypical society in which this can happen, and this is the liturgy. In the eucharist, the individual "projects" of each member are resolved and reconciled in Christ: Christ is the living unity which resides in the interior of each subjectivity, the whole community present simultaneously within each member of it, and fully available simultaneously to each member. Christ, to use Sartre's expression,[1] is a "here-everywhere", the constitutive unity of the group fully present and interiorised within each component. The

[1] Quoted in R. D. Laing's *Reason and Violence: a Decade of Sartre's Philosophy*, London.

individual projects are reconciled within a whole project—Christ—which transcends each individual member and yet is fully present within him. Each member of the group encounters Christ as the centre of the subjectivity of the other, and as the centre of his own subjectivity, so that there is no more possibility of one man objectifying and exploiting another than there is of a man objectifying and exploiting himself. In this situation, the real depth of meaning in "do unto others as you would have them do unto you" is clear: our relationship with others is to resemble our relationship with ourself in the sense that our self-relationship is one of subject to subject: we can never fully objectify ourselves. This is to be the prototype of our relation to others: the basis of community is a reciprocity of subjects, each interiorising the subjective, free self of the other and being mutually interiorised. As Christians we see that this is possible because, if we really live Christ's life, we, as Christ, are encountering Christ in the other: the relationship is that of a self-encounter, and this is why it cannot be one of exploitation. When Christ told us that what we did to others we did to him, he meant that he was to be the interiorised ground of that reciprocity of subjectivities which constitutes human community.

To put it this way is to risk obscurantism for the sake of trying to translate what the gospels say into effective political action. The terms we are using here are Sartre's, who is describing, as an atheistic Marxist, an idea of community which is integral to Christianity and traditional Christian theology. We need to build a political society where the unity of the whole community can be interiorised within each member of it, where individual subjects are both reconciled in face-to-face relationship, between themselves, and, in and through this, reconciled into a whole community. This last point is very important: the reconciliation of two persons, in direct relationship, must share in and be partly constituted by the whole reconciliation of men in the complete community. When we respond to each other, in the liturgy, we are responding to the whole community in each other. A face-to-face relationship, simply by being most intensely itself, must point beyond itself to the wider community from which it springs and which is its ground. We can go back, briefly, to the image of the marriage community: here the direct relationship of husband and wife comes to live in terms of the whole community of the family: when the couple are most completely present to each other as man and wife, they are present to each other as the ground of a community, the parents of their children. We can go back, too, to what we began by saying about Christ's involvement in any act of human communication which establishes community: Christ is the ground of the communication, and the communication is directed outwards to him, sharing in him, simply by being itself, a human interchange. Personal relationships within community remain absolutely valuable in themselves, while being simultaneously part of a depth beyond themselves. De Rougement commented that two people in love were not two people looking at each other but two people looking in the same direction; we need to adapt this image by saying that two people in love are two people who, *through* looking directly at each other, are looking in the same direction, and the difficulty of finding any adequate physical image for this is less important than the need to affirm it. Coleridge compared the state, in a brilliant image, to a portrait which seems to be looking at each man individually while looking at them all; Sartre would recognise this as a metaphor of community, as the Christian recognises it, also, as a metaphor of Christ.

We have said that to live authentically is to live the life of human community and therefore the life of Christ. To make an authentic act of personal self-affirmation is thus to affirm the human community and Christ: to be most purely oneself is to point beyond oneself. In *The Courage To Be*, Paul Tillich points out how this is so: how, in affirming himself as an authentic individual, a man is affirming himself as communal, affirming what it is to be human. We can contrast this interestingly with what Sartre has to say about the nature of authentic individual action and self-affirmation in *Existentialism and Humanism*. For Sartre, the *angst* involved in any human choice and action is that it is, inevitably, a way of defining others in the process of defining myself. If there is no "given" human nature, any personal act is a deepening of the definition of what it means to be human, and is therefore a way of binding and committing others: if as an existentialist I choose to go to war, I am creating a human possibility and making a human statement, and as a result I am affecting the actions and choices of others, even if this is not my intention. To act authentically, as a free man, is thus to infringe the freedom of others, to specify more clearly for them what being human can mean, to pose them with new choices and commitments. For Sartre, this is part of a whole preoccupation with the way the exercise of personal freedom can enslave another simply by being itself, without conscious intention: this relates, clearly, to much of what we have already said about clashing human projects. But this is one point at which the Christian and existentialist differ. For the Christian, the only definition of what it is to be human is Christ, who is at the centre of the reality of all men; to affirm myself, as an individual, is thus to affirm the whole human race, in him. I affirm this simply by being myself; for Sartre, simply to be oneself is to risk binding others, disrupting their freedom. In Christ, the conflict of individual projects and self-definitions is resolved: he is at the root of all authentic life, fully personal yet fully shared.

Tillich sees any such act of authentic self-affirmation as essentially an act of self-forgiveness, self-acceptance. When a man is gripped by guilt he cannot make this act, he is sunk in neurosis. "Neurosis is the way of avoiding non-being by avoiding being": the man who is frightened of encountering himself is inauthentic, settling for half, refusing to risk tragedy and thus incapable of self-achievement. Schizophrenia, Laing says, is a way of being dead to avoid being killed. To face the possibility of tragedy is to push through into a new authenticity, and this, because it is an affirmation of Christ, is both a self-reconciliation and a reconciliation with all men, all creation:

> I am content to follow to its source
> Every event in action or in thought;
> Measure the lot; forgive myself the lot!
> When such as I cast out remorse
> So great a sweetness flows into the breast
> We must laugh and we must sing,
> We are blessed by everything,
> Everything we look upon is blessed.

Yeats knew that to penetrate himself to the core, to face the ultimate reality of what he was, was to break through tragedy and guilt into a wild and total self-affirmation. At the root of the artist's life is a fellowship with all life: when

Yeats says that "the artist's joy is of one substance with that of sanctity", he means that to be holy is to be whole, to live that wholeness of life which springs from the reconciliation of all things in Christ. To follow all life to its source, to push commitment and exploration through to the end, is to know the wholeness of the crucifixion and resurrection of Christ: to be most weak is to be most strong.

Yeats's sense of fellowship with all life is directly Christian: "The sympathy with all living things, sinful and righteous alike, which the imaginative arts awaken, is that forgiveness of sins commanded by Christ." The joyful life of the imagination demands a responsive entry into all life, as the poet and novelist and dramatist has to feel his way, inwardly, into every quality of life in his work. Christianity, as Yeats points out, involves a responsiveness to all kinds of life, of every kind of moral quality; it is a condition in which we are blessed by everything. This, at a fairly abstract level, has been a traditional Christian belief: all things proclaim Christ just by being, all things were made through and in him, and the church is the way he makes all creation his own. What we have largely failed to do is to realise at the level of ordinary moral behaviour that Christianity is about community and not judgement, as Stanley Windass has pointed out:

In the New Testament language, the acknowledgement of oneself as a "sinner", like the

publican in the Temple, is the acknowledgement of the truth about human nature, which
forms the basis of a new fellowship, and is the
ground of that existential humility which
Christ continuously teaches by word and deed.

It is only by the full recognition and acceptance
of a community of guilt, in other words, that we
can break through to a community of forgiveness.
To recognise oneself as a sinner is not to condemn oneself, cast oneself out of community: it
is the ground on which community can be built:

> We know we must not say "raca" to the enemy
> outside, but we are continuously saying "raca"
> to the enemy within; and in this again we live
> a contradiction, for the community is in each
> of us and each of us in the community, so that
> it is impossible to dissociate our attitude to
> others from our attitude to the constituent
> parts of our own personalities. To condemn
> ourselves is to commit an act of violence
> against ourselves, to reject and cast out, as by
> exorcism, the "shadow" of unacknowledged
> impulse.[1]

It is obvious how close this is to what we have
already said about the nature of human community. If my identity as a person is inseparable
from others, I damage others in damaging myself; if community is a reciprocity of identity, I

[1] Stanley Windass, "Sin", *Slant* 5 (Summer 1965), 25–6.

must have that kind of respect for my own self-hood which I should have for others. The success of a marriage can turn not so directly on how much I respect my wife as on how much I respect myself, since I see myself continually mirrored in her, inseparable from what it is to be her, and it is thus impossible for me to love her unless I can love myself: if I can live with myself, the chances are I can live with someone else. The instinct to hurt someone we love when we are disgusted with ourselves also comes from this reciprocity: hurting someone close to me is a way of punishing myself.

The real danger involved in entering sympathetically into all life is one well known to the artist: it is the danger of risking a loss of identity, of moral commitment. Keats felt his power of "negative capability", his ability to feel his way into all life, as this kind of self-annihilation: when he entered a room full of people he felt his personality crushed, when he saw a sparrow pecking around on the window-sill he became the sparrow and pecked around with it, losing his identity. To become everything is to risk being nothing: Keats felt this power as a barrier to becoming a person, with a hard core of commitment and identity.

The problem is central to the novels of George Eliot. In *Adam Bede*, the severely principled, moral Adam has to learn to unbend, to experience flexible human sympathy; it is this flexibility which Eliot sees as being at the root of the novelist's own achievement:

> These fellow-mortals, every one, must be accepted as they are: you can neither straighten their noses, nor brighten their wit, nor rectify their dispositions; and it is these people—amongst whom your life is passed— that it is needful you should tolerate, pity and love: it is these more or less ugly, stupid, inconsistent peoples whose movements of goodness you should be able to admire—for whom you should cherish all possible hopes, all possible patience. And I would not, even if I had the choice, be the clever novelist who could create a world so much better than this, in which we get up in the morning to do our daily work, that you would be likely to turn a harder, colder eye on the dusty streets and the common green fields—on the real, breathing men and women, who can be chilled by your indifference or injured by your prejudice; who can be cheered and helped onward by your fellow-feeling, your forebearance, your outspoken, brave justice.[1]

The novel, as Eliot sees it, is not to be concerned primarily with heroes, or "the sublimest abstract of all clerical graces", but with shaping the flow and recoil of common human sympathy: the novelist has the peculiar power of being able

[1] George Eliot, *Adam Bede*, bk. 2, ch. 17.

to enter into the lives of all his characters, and to understand every kind of consciousness as a response within a whole pattern. This is essentially what Eliot does in *Middlemarch*: by seeing society as a web of interlacing points of consciousness, a complex meshing of personal versions of seeing, she can trace the interlocking of characters and events from every viewpoint. We are reminded constantly that events are never the same when observed as when lived; that the reality of an event unfolds only in the consciousness of all those it involves; that the "lights and shades" of reality fall in a different pattern within each consciousness. It is the novelist, gifted simultaneously with the responsive sympathy to explore every consciousness, and the intellectual power, penetrating this, to see the *whole* pattern of events and relationships within which consciousness moves, who holds the key to reality; he must combine, somehow, the essential liberalism of this total, sympathetic seeing with a personal identity, a mind with its own moral atmosphere and commitment.

But the balance is difficult to find, and Eliot's own description of Daniel Deronda shows that she is aware of the problem:

> His early-wakened sensibility and reflective-ness had developed into a many-sided sympathy, which threatened to hinder any persistent course of action ... A too reflective

and diffuse sympathy was in danger of para-
lysing in him that indignation against wrong
and that selectness of fellowship which are the
conditions of moral force.[1]

Liberal sympathy can lead too easily to what
Eliot calls elsewhere in the novel a "bird's-eye
reasonableness", which cripples committed
action. To move away from the simple moral
principle and action of an Adam Bede towards
a more complex, less narrow morality, is perhaps
to lose that rooted strength of positive life which
Adam has. In *Middlemarch*, the artist who can
enter sympathetically into all life is Will
Ladislaw, the light-hearted cosmopolitan whose
broad vision comes dangerously near to a lack of
moral seriousness; it is with Dorothea, the
woman of intense if potentially dangerous moral
commitment, that Eliot's chief sympathies lie.
In this novel, and in *The Mill on the Floss*, one
possible resolution of the tension is explored in
the idea of martyrdom, self-sacrifice. The martyr
is one who gains an intense moral identity
through total self-surrender to others, someone
who makes this entry into others' lives the
ground of her own self-achievement as a person.
But there are dangers in this, too: Maggie
Tulliver in *The Mill on the Floss*, and Dorothea
in *Middlemarch*, are both threatened as persons
with what Will Ladislaw calls "the fanaticism of

[1] George Eliot, *Daniel Deronda*, bk. 4, ch. 32.

sympathy": to make an intense cult of dissolving away into others can be as destructive as making an intense cult of egoism. Dinah Morris, the young Methodist in *Adam Bede*, is perhaps intended as a point of balance—she is a woman with tender, common sympathy and yet intense moral conviction, a working girl and a prophet. But the achievement here is marred by an idealisation which suggests Eliot's eagerness to achieve a fusion, rather than her success in actually doing so.

For the Christian, this remains a crucial problem. If to be authentically myself is to be in community with others, is there a point at which sympathy with others becomes a kind of self-betrayal? How can we regain the sense of authentic, responsive life which Yeats's verse captures without surrendering to mere liberal compromise, a bird's-eye morality which is concerned with being nice to everyone, rather than with truth and commitment? How are we to be inwardly sympathetic to men who drop A-bombs and operate policies which prevent millions of people all over the world from living real human lives? What is being a Christian to feel like in a world which demands uncompromising, revolutionary force and energy before it is converted to Christ? We are not alone in this difficulty, of course: the paradox of destroying oneself and community in the attempt to build community is one of the central paradoxes of recent history.

The christian has to make some kind of commitment, within this situation. We have to decide whether we are the kind of radical who is prepared to use almost any weapon to bring about justice, or whether we believe that the way the justice comes is part of its meaning; if this is our position, we have to ask ourselves whether, in believing that we can establish a Christian society without dirtying our hands, we are merely making a stock liberal underestimation of what it will take to build that society. Part of the answer is there already, perhaps, in the whole situation of Christians in the world, in the relation between world and liturgy: to make a Christian society is not to begin from scratch, but to *extend* what we believe already exists as a real fact in the liturgical community. We begin from the future, as it exists now in the liturgy, and make this live in the present. What kind of struggle making it live will entail is uncertain: at the moment we are still exploring the meaning of being part of this special community, and a good deal of Christian energy is devoted simply to this. But the problem can never be really separate from the question of what society we are to create: the relation between world and liturgy is two-way, for it is through our ordinary insight into politics, literature, psychology, that we begin to understand the meanings of the liturgical community. If the church is to help create a common culture, it needs all the resources of our present culture—not as weapons at its disposal, but as ways of understanding the world, and therefore itself. What we can do at present, perhaps, is to work towards the development of a common language—to begin to build that linguistic community between church and world which has been absent for so long. By trying to make our meanings intelligible to ourselves, we might find eventually that they have become intelligible to others.